Thanks Be To
God

Thanks Be To
God

P̲RAYERS AND PARABLES FOR

PUBLIC WORSHIP

Glen E. Rainsley

THE
PILGRIM
PRESS
Cleveland

DEDICATION

*T*his book is dedicated – in general – to all who plan, lead or participate in worship. I hope it inspires your creativity, enhances your leadership, and contributes to your enjoyment of God.

This book is dedicated – in particular – to Susan, my wife, and Abby, my daughter. I offer thanks for their encouragement through the trials of writing and the frustrations of dealing with our computer. I hope that sales of this book will help provide books for Abby at college.

This book is dedicated – in a footnote – to Tiger Lily (cat) and Keebler (chinchilla), whose furry friendship keeps me in touch with God's creation.

The Pilgrim Press, 700 Prospect Avenue, Cleveland, Ohio 44115
thepilgrimpress.com
© 2005 by Glen E. Rainsley

Biblical quotations are from the New Revised Standard Version of the Bible © copyright 1989 by the Division of Christian Education of the National Council of the Churches of Christ in the U.S.A., and are used by permission.

10 09 08 07 06 05   5 4 3 2 1

Library of Congress Cataloging-in-Publication Data
Rainsley, Glen E.
      Thanks be to God : prayers and parables for public worship /
   Glen E.Rainsley.
         p.   cm.
      Includes index.
      ISBN 0-8298-1637-2 (pbk. : alk. paper)
      1. Public worship.   2. Worship programs.   3. Church bulletins.
4. Prayers.   I. Title.
BV10.3.R35   2005
264'.13—dc22

2005041932

Contents

Introduction

There is no finer thing we do as human beings than to engage in worship. This is a bold statement, but I do have my reasons for making it...

✛ Worship is an apt response to the commandments Jesus gave highest priority (see Mark 12:28-31). Through worship we express our love for God, and through worship we gain inspiration to activate/enact love of neighbor.

✛ Worship invites us to use our God-given talents in music, art, verbal expression and physical movement.

✛ Worship enriches us with a range of access routes to experiencing connectedness with God and with one another, from the practices of silent prayer and solitary reflection to the congregational participation of full corporate worship.

✛ Worship is the venue in which common life and spiritual realm have a close point of contact. We might characterize worship as mystical and mundane. Years ago, I invited parishioners to consider their place in the sanctuary as holy ground, and I mounted a sign at the exit door that read "Service Entrance" to remind them that faith must be borne into the world of everyday life.

This book offers resources for worship. It is intended to equip lay and clergy worship leaders, and it is designed to invite use as a companion in personal devotions. The categories of worship materials included cover the common elements of corporate worship [calls to worship, opening prayers, words of assurance, prayers of dedication, benedictions and pastoral prayers]. I hope that my samples/examples inspire readers to exercise their own spiritual creativity.

Two sections of the book merit particular note. "Prayers for Special Occasions" offers resources that can be used at times of specific focus or need. The prayers are identified in a manner that makes usage clear. "Parables" is a collection of pieces that derive their form and messages from the teaching methods of Jesus. The introduction to this section of the book serves to provide a more complete explanation of the purpose behind the parables.

Although I have supplied ample resources for the Advent/Christmas season (to get readers up and running for the start of the church year!), the majority of materials is intended for the weeks designated as "common" or "ordinary" time. Liturgically, we celebrate worship during these weeks between Pentecost and Advent with the color green, the color of living plants, of creation's bounty. I like to think of this period in the church — precisely half the calendar year — as a time for recognizing the connection between divine presence and human creativity. Green speaks of newness, growth, generative possibility.

For resources related to specific days and seasons of the liturgical year, I refer readers to the many fine books that contain such material. Among these, I especially suggest *Hear Our Prayer*, a book I wrote in 1996 for United Church Press. (Although this book is technically out of print, you may obtain it from me by e-mail request at rainsleybooks@yahoo.com. A $15.00 check will cover both book and shipping.)

Use this book. Enjoy its contents. And savor worship...for the love of God.

CALLS TO WORSHIP

The call at the start of worship serves as a wake-up and a welcome. I do not mean that it functions as a mechanism for startling into alertness anyone dozing in the sanctuary. The call is simply a beckoning to awaken spiritually to the presence of God. It extends the invitation to enter into God's realm, a place of open welcome to all.

Some time ago, at the request of a grandmother, I gave a church sanctuary tour to a seven-year-old who had never been in a church building. I did my best to explain what he was seeing and touching, let him try the organ, and described what he might expect on Sunday when he would attend his first worship service. When that day came, people greeted one another and settled in, the organist played the prelude, and I arose to speak. The child spoke first. He said, loud enough for all to hear, "Hey, I like this place!" What a terrific call to worship, I thought to myself. It was a perfectly acceptable revoicing of the psalmist's words, "I was glad when they said to me, 'Let us go to the house of God.'"

The tone of that child's message is one to capture in any call to worship. It is indeed a good thing to be together in any place where we share and celebrate the love of God.

The clamor of the marketplace, the clashing sounds of conflict and the distressing cries of famine, the noise of our own wheels spinning…sometimes these are so loud that we do not hear the voice of the Prince of Peace.

The thick skin of emotional toughness, the avoidance of any vulnerability, the desire to armor ourselves against possible hurts or pains…sometimes these are so built up that we do not feel the touch of the One called Wonderful Counselor.

The jumble of media faces selling to us but not caring for us, the expressions of loneliness roundabout, the look we have when nothing is going quite right…sometimes these are so apparent that we do not see the smile on the face of the Savior we love.

This morning we have come to pay attention to the One who is Prince of Peace, Wonderful Counselor, beloved Savior. Welcome to worship.

✤ Advent
✤ Jesus, nature of
✤ Faith, attentiveness to

Leader: How difficult to wait for the joy we know is coming…
People: The gift from God, Emmanuel.
Leader: How hard to imagine the wonder of God's love…
People: A manger-born babe, a sovereign to be.
Leader: How demanding to prepare for a living presence…
People: The Messiah in our midst, the hope of humankind.
All: We gather as people learning to wait patiently, trying to imagine boldly, striving to prepare faithfully. Through the work and worship of Christ's church, we live in the spirit of Advent.

✤ Advent
✤ Anticipation
✤ God, gifts of

Leader: We await what God will deliver to us…
People: A Child who is vulnerable to the world's ills and open to its wonders.
Leader: We await what God will provide to us…
People: A Sovereign whose people we are and whose way of governance is the rule of love.
Leader: We await what God will send us…
People: A Counselor who offers comfort, inspires courage, and leads the way to wholeness.
Leader: We await what God will grant to us…
People: A Savior who brings peace and forgiveness, the gifts of grace.

All: We await with joy the coming of Emmanuel – Mary's baby and Sovereign over all, bearer of comfort and source of salvation.

✤ Advent
✤ God, gifts of
✤ Isaiah 9

When we hear the words, "I am coming to stay with you awhile," our reactions vary depending upon who it is who utters those words.

Is it a friend whose conversation and fellowship we treasure? Our reaction – joy.

Is it a casual acquaintance who loves the attractions of the area and who finds us to be the cheapest motel? Our reaction – disgust.

Is it a family member related to us not only by genetic ties but also by bonds of love? Our reaction – warmth.

Is it a person whose ill-tempered and massive, messy dog is a constant companion? Our reaction – apprehension.

"I am coming to stay with you awhile." This first Sunday of Advent, we realize anew every year that is what God says to us in announcing the impending birth of Jesus. What is our reaction to that? Today and through the Advent season, may our worship encourage fitting response to the promising presence of our God who chooses to be with us.

✤ Advent (first Sunday)
✤ Anticipation
✤ God, presence of

(Based upon Isaiah 9)
Leader: This world of ours can perceive anew the presence of God within it…can know it…can feel it in a way that is personal and universal, comforting and hopeful. But how?
People: Unto us a child is born.
Leader: And how to put a name to the presence of God in our midst? God addresses our needs in so many ways.…
We need wise direction and divine guidance.

People: Wonderful Counselor.
Leader: We need strength and creative power.
People: Mighty God.
Leader: We need sure and certain sustenance.
People: Everlasting Father.
Leader: We need a source of forgiveness and reconciliation and trust.
People: Prince of Peace.
Leader: How great and loving our God to provide for this world according to its needs, for we receive at Christmas the perfect gift for all our occasions and circumstances, the presence of a living Savior. Rejoice and celebrate!
All: "For unto us a child is born. And his name shall be called Wonderful Counselor, Mighty God, Everlasting Father, Prince of Peace." Glory be to God.

✤ Advent (fourth Sunday)
✤ God, gifts of
✤ Isaiah 9

Leader: In the praise of song and the petitions of prayer, in the community's convening of receptive spirits and the heart's hearing of God's Word,
People: Our faith takes form as worship.
Leader: [Fill in a description of mission efforts in which the congregation is engaged. For example: in the collecting of clothing and the distributing of food, in the building of homes and the pursuing of justice.]
People: Our faith takes form as service.
Leader: In the recognition of forgiveness and the celebration of fellowship, in the breaking of bread and the sharing of a cup,
People: Our faith takes form as sacrament.
All: We give thanks this morning for a faith tangible in form as the Christ who was its Source and remains its Sustainer.

✤ Advent (communion)
✤ Communion
✤ Faith, form of

Leader: When we open our doors to all seekers and sojourners,

People: When we open our hearts to the teachings of truth and the beckonings of faith,

Leader: When we put aside all judgmental thoughts and envy,

People: When we put aside the selfishness that wounds and the enmity that destroys,

Leader: When we dare to envision all peoples as one and at peace,

People: When we dare to trust the potency of compassion and to practice the privilege of service,

All: The love of God is at home within us, our worship comes alive with joy, and the coming Messiah finds a welcome within us.

✤ Advent
✤ Faith, traits of
✤ God, love of

Leader: This Christmas Sunday our spirits are ready to receive the blessed news first heard in the Bethlehem hills.

People: We listen for heavenly voices proclaiming the Messiah's birth.

Leader: This Christmas Sunday our spirits are eager to see the child who was, for visitors to the manger, a wonder to behold.

People: We look for places where the Light of this world shines forth.

Leader: This Christmas Sunday our spirits are prepared to worship God who chose to reveal in person the ways of grace and goodness.

People: We labor for the growth of faith's understanding and for the maturing of a true partnership with Christ.

Leader: This Christmas Sunday our spirits are primed to celebrate the arrival of love incarnate, the holy and humble Child.

People: We love with boldness in the Child's name, and we dare to hope for the strength to love far beyond this season.

All: Glory be to God on high! Glory be to the Bethlehem Child!

✤ Advent (fourth Sunday)
✤ Anticipation
✤ Faith, traits of

Leader: This night through a story's unfolding, a holy love
embraces us.
People: We gather to hear the story of our Savior's birth.
Leader: This night brings an unwrapping of hopes long held
within.
People: We gather to open ourselves to the promises of God.
Leader: This night we need angelic instructions and we follow
the starlight's guidance.
People: We gather as one family drawn together by the Messiah
in a manger.
All: We gather to greet the world's Light, the newborn
Christ.

✤ Christmas Eve
✤ Jesus, Light of the world
✤ God, promises of

Leader: There were pronouncements by prophets, God's promises to keep, prayer-prompting statements that foretold
a day when all people could say...
People: Christ the Savior is born!
Leader: There were sounds in the sky, and angels starred that
night speaking wondrous good news to shepherds
stunned and startled to hear...
People: Christ the Savior is born!
Leader: There was a dim stable in the city of David where
devoted parents and drowsy-eyed animals first felt the
presence we celebrate and proclaim...
People: Christ the Savior is born!
All: We come in good faith to rejoice in our Savior's birth.

✤ Christmas Eve
✤ Christmas
✤ God, promises of

Leader: With the heavens star-dappled and angel-strewn,
People: We sense the majesty and might of God on high.
Leader: Through the travel-worn couple and the stable-born Child,
People: We sense the glory and holiness of God's humble arrival in human form.
Leader: In the candlelight service of worship this evening and the Christ-inspired service of mission to others in days ahead,
People: We sense the wonder and joy of God's Spirit moving in our midst.
All: As we gather together our God draws near, and we feel our faith as sustaining power and hearty good cheer.

✤ Christmas Eve
✤ Christmas Eve candlelight worship
✤ God, nature of

Leader: Though Jesus entered this world centuries ago,
People: His presence in our lives remains timely and timeless.
Leader: Though Jesus made his earthly home in a place far distant,
People: His presence dwells in the community of the faithful and in the hearts of us all.
Leader: Though angels from the realms of glory delivered the announcement of Jesus' birth,
People: It is we who translate the reality of his presence into the impact of action and the form of faith.
All: We experience our Christ as an immediate, indwelling, inspiring presence that draws us together for worship and service.

✤ Christmastide
✤ Jesus, nature of
✤ Faith, components of

Leader: Just this morning, the Creator has drawn forth the sun from below the horizon to give light to a new day.
People: All praise and thanks to God.

Leader: Just this morning, the Christ has come into our midst, for we are many gathered in one place.
People: All praise and thanks to God.
Leader: Just this morning, the Spirit has given us breath and voice to shape into prayer and song.
People: All praise and thanks to God.
Leader: Already this morning God has done great things in our lives.
People: We lift up our hearts in joy and gratitude as we worship our gracious God.

✤ God, worship of
✤ God, praise to
✤ Worship, newness and joy of

Leader: In times of difficult decision, we can feel as though we dwell in a wilderness place where temptations recur and concerns about self-preservation bedevil us.
People: In these times and always, we call upon our steadfast God.
Leader: In times of personal struggle, we can feel as though we dwell in a wilderness place where material needs present themselves sharply and spiritual resources get depleted.
People: In these times and always, we call upon our steadfast God.
Leader: In times of having no sense of direction, we can feel as though we dwell in a wilderness place where our choices matter little and our destination seems unclear.
People: In these times and always, we call upon our steadfast God.
Leader: It is God who used the wilderness to shape a people of faith and to prepare Jesus for the demanding course of ministry in this world.
People: We place our trust in God's power as we offer our praise.

✤ Lent
✤ Wilderness
✤ God, steadfastness of

Leader: This season of Lent, we give thanks for a past filled with trials and triumphs, challenges and changes, fond remembrances and forgiveness received.

People: We offer our gratitude and praise for the blessing of continuity.

Leader: This season of Lent, we give thanks for a present filled with sacrament and service, programs and prayers, coffee-hour conversations and covenant commitments.

People: We offer our gratitude and praise for the treasure of life together.

Leader: This season of Lent, we give thanks for a future filled with possibilities and promise, vitality and vision, emerging ministries and exciting movement.

People: We offer our gratitude and praise for the opportunity to do God's will as the Spirit reveals it and enables it.

All: We worship the God who has gifted our past, who guards our present, who will guide our future.

✤ Lent
✤ God, gratitude to
✤ God, steadfastness of

Leader: At day's dawning, we slip from sleep into alertness, and we scan the possibilities of time ahead.

People: Thanks be to God for this good life.

Leader: Amidst the day's doings, we experience the variety of labor and recreation, and we identify ways to use our gifts.

People: Thanks be to God for this good life.

Leader: When day is done, we pause for recollection and reflection, and in our wisest moments we acknowledge that grace alone has sustained us.

People: Thanks be to God for this good life.

All: We bring to our time of worship awakened spirits, hands willingly offered in service, and hearts grateful beyond measure. Glory be to God.

✤ Lent (evening worship)
✤ Life, goodness of
✤ God, steadfastness of

Leader: We have gotten into shoes this morning after a night of unshod slumber.

People: We awake to celebrate the new day that is God's gift to us.

Leader: We have gotten into vehicles this morning and have come here from many points of origin.

People: We travel to this place in order to share with one another a portion of the journey of faith.

Leader: We have gotten into pews this morning and have prepared ourselves for worship.

People: We come together in a holy space that is both sanctuary and classroom for our spirits.

All: This day of palms, this day of Jesus' journey into Jerusalem, we gather as a family of persons ready to serve God, willing to follow Christ, able to receive the Spirit's power.

✣ Palm Sunday
✣ Faith, journey of
✣ Worship, preparation for

We have gathered tonight as disciples. Within us we have capacities like those of the twelve: to deny, to betray, to doubt...and, yes, to trust, to honor, to believe. Tonight we sit together to share supper with Jesus of Nazareth, a Person we have come to know as teacher and friend and more...as God's own Child and chosen One.

It is Thursday tonight. It is a time of closeness with Jesus when we sense at the table, as never before, the costs and joys of discipleship.

This is the final night of a life. It is the eve of the unthinkable, yet the prelude of a promise.

Let us join together now in sharing the simple prayer Jesus taught to his disciples when they asked him how to pray. The words are both his and ours.

[the prayer of Jesus]

✣ Maundy Thursday
✣ Discipleship, costs and joys of
✣ Discipleship, traits of

We come here in the darkness of the night to remember One whose presence and actions enlightened the world. We will be participating in the events that led from the joyous fellowship of the Passover meal through bitter moments of friendship cut short and discipleship gone astray. Words such as betrayal, denial, crucifixion and death tell the final portions of the story of Jesus. For those whose hopes were alive with the One called the Light, the times grew dreary and depressing as the forces of darkness seemed to extinguish that Light once and for all.

[an opening prayer may follow]

❖ Maundy Thursday
❖ Jesus, final meal with disciples
❖ Discipleship

Leader: Evil and death had their day and wielded their power; this day we celebrate the triumph of goodness and new life. By the grace and power of God, He is risen!
People: Christ is risen indeed!
Leader: Though love had seemed defeated, though events had suggested a divine desertion, this day we have reason to rejoice and to exult in our faith. By the grace and power of God, He is risen!
People: Christ is risen indeed!
Leader: Christ is risen!
People: May joy be ours this Easter day! Glory be to God!

❖ Easter
❖ Jesus, resurrection of
❖ God, glory to

Leader: As a child, Jesus astounded the scholars in the temple with his knowledge and wisdom.
People: We come to worship the One known to us as Teacher.
Leader: During his travels, Jesus often released from illness the sick or diseased.
People: We come to worship the One known to us as Healer.
Leader: In situation after situation, Jesus affirmed the worth of persons deemed worthless and helped identify their gifts.

People: We come to worship the One known to us as Enabler.
Leader: Throughout his ministry, Jesus freed folks from the bondage of grief and sin.
People: We come to worship the One known to us as Redeemer.
Leader: Beyond crucifixion and death, Jesus lived to reveal God's power and love.
All: We come to worship Jesus the Christ.

♣ Eastertide
♣ Jesus, nature of
♣ Worship, newness and joy of

Leader: We can sense God as Creator in the warmth of the sun, the bite of the wind, the floral smells we can almost taste.
People: We can feel God as Presence in special places that move us to reverence, in times of prayer that impress us as holy moments.
Leader: We can appreciate God as Provider in the caring acts of others who minister to us, through the responses we make to the needs of others as we are drawn to minister to them.
All: But we can most fully understand and love God through the person of a Person, through Jesus called the Christ, the Child of God. It is as followers in fellowship with the Teacher of Nazareth that we come together to worship God this day.

♣ God, nature of
♣ Jesus, as revealer of God
♣ God, sensing

*T*he absolute enemy of humor is predictability. Foreknowledge of a punch-line ruins any joke. And nobody enjoys hearing a comedian whose routines are routine. Humor is the product of creativity and surprise. Can we not then see humor as a central attribute of our God? For God is the Creator *par excellence,* who provides us with an evolving world that challenges our imaginations to a quest and rewards our curiosity with the discovery of miracles. And God is the generator of surprise, loving us in unpredictable yet reliably stead-fast ways – as in the Exodus, the Bethlehem birth, the resurrection event.

We gather to worship our God who is Creator and generator of surprise throughout our past and in every moment when we are amazed by grace and so prompted to joy and to laughter. The psalmist said, "I was *glad* when they said to me, 'Let us go to the house of God.'" This is indeed a place and a time for gladness.

❖ Worship, newness and joy of
❖ Humor
❖ God, as Creator

*I*n the morning of each day, as we awaken to the buzz or ring of an alarm or to the gentle promptings of an internal clock, as we hes-itate to confront the air outside our blanket cocoon, as we bring the world into focus with eyes that have watched a night-long festival of dreams, as we trundle off to face the horrible honesty of the bath-room mirror...in the morning of each day, may our first thoughts be thanks to God for the new life of a new day.

During the course of each day, in the attention we pay to those around us, in the labors of muscle and mind that our vocations require, in the activities that fill our retirement...during the course of each day may our gratitude deepen toward the God who joins with us in work and play.

At the evening of each day, as we reconvene the family, as we reflect upon or share our stories over macaroni and cheese, as we settle solo into a TV sitcom or snuggle up with a good book...at the evening of each day may our thoughts turn toward God whose pres-ence sustains us in waking hours and in promised sleep.

This morning we gather on the first day of the week to worship our God. In the week ahead, let worship continue each day long, and may we live to the glory of God.

❖ God, steadfastness of
❖ Worship, newness and joy of
❖ Time, God's presence within

Leader: We gather to worship because we value the connection with God provided by a faith that has taken shape over millennia.

People: We gather to worship because we need the spiritual support of a community to make honest assessment of whether or not our faith is fit and in good shape.

Leader: We gather to worship because we rely upon God to help us shape a vision of things to come.

All: We worship the one true God who, as Sovereign over all time, is our Creator, Sustainer and Redeemer.

✤ Worship, purposes of
✤ God, nature of
✤ Worship, newness and joy of

Leader: Springtime triggers a renovation of the natural world, a coloring of the landscape with subtle greens of unfurling leaves and vibrant hues of flowers in bloom.

People: May our time of worship inspire renewal of our spirits, the blossoming of belief and the coloring of all we do with bold commitment.

Leader: Springtime pushes us toward cleaning the inside of our homes, toward getting outdoors to do planting and yard work.

People: May our time of worship lead us toward inner order and peace, toward reaching out in good faith as we plant seeds of hope and pledge to do the work of nurture.

All: In this springtime of the Spirit, we sense the warmth of God's love and we feel a great potential for growing in faith.

✤ Seasons (spring)
✤ Faith, growth of
✤ Faith, traits of

[Note: The following call to worship is something of a template to be adapted to the user's own environment.]

𝒜t this time of year a ripening of spring comes to this area.

There are reliable indicators of the season's presence: the splutter and whine of power mowers on weekend afternoons, the popping forth of seedlings in the vegetable garden, the urge to roller skate or fly a kite, the longing for picnics and hikes and Frisbee tosses.

There are beautiful signs of the season's renewing power: the greening to fullness of branches above, the sequence of wildflower colors that spot the fields and roadsides, the flash of feeding trout, the lingering light of a late pink sunset.

There are transforming moments in this season: the humbling careless slip in a mud puddle, the aerobic exercise of gnat-swatting, the noise of traffic and outdoor conversations downtown, the choral night-sound of peepers.

This time of year has its reliable indicators, beautiful signs, transforming moments, but these go for naught if they do not bring a mature spring season to our spirits by reminding us that our God is reliable as Sovereign of us and of all, that our God is beautiful in grace and glory, that our God is transforming through acts of justice and love.

May the Spirit ever and always spring to life in our midst.

✤ Seasons (spring)
✤ God, nature of
✤ Environment

Leader: Looking left and right, behind and before,
People: We see our brothers and sisters in faith.
Leader: They are bratty and well-behaved, outgoing and shy, discerning and dull, joyous and despairing. [Other attributes may be added.]
People: They are who we are, children of God striving to live out the love of Christ.
Leader: During this time of worship, upon this day of annual meeting,
People: We offer thanks to God for this family.
Leader: As we congregate, we celebrate, for the gifts are many and the opportunities to serve abound.

All: By the grace of God we gather; to the glory of God we voice our praise.

❖ Community
❖ Discipleship
❖ Church (annual meeting)

Leader: Into this world came One who formed it in its beginnings, who lived in it to teach God's ways and to proclaim good news. This was Jesus, who is known to us

People: As the Teacher from Nazareth, as the Word of creative power.

Leader: Into this world came One who nourished in spirit all he met, who sat at the table with the rejected and neglected of society. This was Jesus, who is known to us

People: As the Teacher from Nazareth, as the Bread of life.

Leader: Into this world came One who loved it completely, who gave to it all that could be given, even the sacrifice of himself. This was Jesus, who is known to us

People: As the Teacher from Nazareth, as the Lamb of God,

All: The One we know as Jesus the Christ. In the name of Christ we gather to offer our praise and ourselves.

❖ Jesus, person of
❖ Jesus, knowledge of
❖ Worship, focus of

There have been times in all our lives when we have unexpectedly caught laughter from someone else. Often it happens at the most awkward moments: in the middle of a wedding or funeral service, at a music recital, during a serious lecture, or at a high-level business meeting. How the laughter starts does not really matter; what is fascinating is that it so readily spreads. If the show tune is correct in stating, "You'll never walk alone," there ought to be an additional verse noting, "You'll never laugh alone." There is something clearly contagious about laughter.

As we gather this morning for worship, we might well consider how much the love of God is like laughter...it is contagious, it is meant to be shared, it comes at surprising times. And although it is often as awkward to spread God's love to a contentious world as it is to spread laughter in serious times, through our worship and

throughout our lives let us strive to be carriers of that love letting
its contagiousness work through us. Welcome to worship.

❧ Humor
❧ God, love of
❧ Mission

Leader: We gather at the bold and bright sounds of instrument
and voice.
People: We come to worship the God of all creation.
Leader: We gather amidst the greetings of friends and strangers.
People: We come to worship the God who makes us all one in
the sharing of our faith.
Leader: We gather in the solitude of reflection and the quiet of
prayer.
People: We come to worship the God whose Word speaks to us
and through us.
All: Praise be to God from whom all blessings flow.

❧ Worship
❧ Church
❧ God, nature of

Leader: These days, when slippery words and shaded truths are
commonplace,
People: We gather to proclaim the honest good news of God's
love for all persons.
Leader: These days, when global divisions abound and internal
stresses take their toll,
People: We gather to share a faith that is the source of healing
and serenity.
Leader: These days, when the demands for justice and commitment and compassion are great,
People: We gather to strengthen ourselves and one another for
the tasks of being a servant people.
All: All thanks to God for gathering us together as the
church. This day we shall strive to proclaim, to share
and to strengthen our faith in Jesus Christ.

❧ Faith, practice of
❧ Justice
❧ Mission

Leader: We come this day to hear the Good News, to take it to heart, to allow its renewing and transforming power to work within us.

People: We gather as children of God thankful for the privilege of worship.

Leader: We come this day to equip ourselves as speakers of Good News, as translators of Word into action, as communicators of Christ's love.

People: We gather as children of God thankful for the power of Spirited service.

Leader: We come this day to seek greater understanding of the Good News, to envision a holy and hopeful future, to imagine the many possible ways we can live out our calling.

People: We gather as children of God thankful for the promise of our faith.

All: On this day that God has made, let us rejoice and be glad in it!

✤ Faith, practice of
✤ Good News
✤ Worship, as motivator

Leader: Whoever people are, whether friends or adversaries, nearby neighbors or distant folks we will never meet,

People: God's love embraces us and them and everyone upon this Earth.

Leader: Whenever people live, whether in days of long ago or times within our remembrance, in this very moment or some unknown tomorrow,

People: God's love extends from the past to the present and throughout the future.

Leader: Wherever people dwell, whether in farming community or teeming city, in hut or hovel or high-rise or split-level,

People: God's love reaches here and there and everywhere.

All: As we gather to worship, we give thanks for the inclusiveness, steadfastness and breadth of our Creator's love for humankind.

✤ God, love of
✤ Community
✤ Inclusiveness

Leader: Whenever we have stood star-staring and feeling small but privileged to be part of the universe, or whenever we have looked intently at the life-bearing wisp of milk-weed seed...we have felt the creative power of God.

People: Whenever we have accomplished what seemed impossible, or whenever we have risen above the trials and burdens and stresses that bring us down... we have experienced the comforting power of God.

Leader: Whenever we have heard the music of heartstrings pulled by the hands of faithfulness, or whenever we have recognized the harmony that comes with attuning our wills to the divine... we have experienced the loving power of God.

People: Whenever we have had our spirits lifted by the songs of the community of faith, or whenever we have been moved by the more-than-ornamental meaning of the cross... we have felt the inspiring power of God.

All: We who gather this day come to acknowledge that our God is great and powerful. We come intending to bring honor and praise through our worship.

✤ God, power of
✤ God, mystery of
✤ Faith, signs of

Leader: To everything a season,
People: And a time to every purpose under heaven.
Leader: Time for relaxed summer sojourns and for scheduled daily school bus rides,
People: For involvement with recreational activities and for immersion in challenging studies.
Leader: Time for setting a solid career course and for veering off in new directions,
People: For establishing firm friendships and for discovering the solace of solitude.

Leader: Time for focusing on wondrous potential and for honestly accepting limits,
People: For appreciating the moment at hand and for contemplating eternity.
All: In all circumstances and through all seasons, we offer our thanks and praise to God.

✣ Education
✣ School, start of
✣ Daily life

No one has no need for God.
Everyone needs everything that God provides.
And so we come seeking...
Forgiveness that restores and renews,
Grace that amazes and enables,
Community that strengthens and supports,
Truth that informs and guides,
Love that redeems and heals.
And God is truly in our midst.

✣ God, need for
✣ Faith, attributes of
✣ Worship

Leader: By the grace of our God who calls us together in worship and in service,
People: We strive to live our faith right where we are.
Leader: So we affirm that for sharing strong traditions and for shaping future values,
People: There is no place better.
Leader: For developing warm companionship and for doing tasks of mission,
People: There is no place better.
Leader: For offering our joys and concerns in prayer and for opening ourselves to God in worship,
People: There is no place better.
Leader: In this church, and wherever people gather to be guided by the Spirit in enacting Christly love,

All: There is no place better. We worship with gladness and thanksgiving.

✤ Church, value of
✤ Faith, practice of
✤ Community

Leader: Whether we have greeted the day with groggy grumbling or have leaped up alert at dawn's first light,
People: Let us praise our God for the opportunities of this life and for the promise of life to come.
Leader: Whether we exercise our talents through efforts in our workplaces or expend our energy in wholesome recreation,
People: Let us praise our God in labor and in leisure.
Leader: Whether we hold to a faith generated by generations of family believers or reach out to grasp a faith newly arrived,
People: Let us praise our God through the celebration of communion in worship and through the creation of community in the world.
All: For all good gifts, our thanks and praise to God.

✤ God, gifts of
✤ Faith, practice of
✤ Daily life

Leader: This time of worship is a personal and private event:
People: We come with individual concerns that move us toward confidential conversations with our God.
Leader: This time of worship is a family reunion:
People: We come to enjoy companionship with persons who are our sisters and brothers in Christ.
Leader: This time of worship is a creation of community:
People: We come to express a common faith in the God who bids us set aside any differences or distractions that hinder our becoming a whole and holy people.
Leader: This time of worship is a foretaste of God's realm:
People: We come to enjoy an acceptance born of Christian love, to sense the presence of the Spirit, to commit ourselves to God's service.

All: We give thanks for this time of shared worship.

✤ Worship, purposes of
✤ Faith, richness of
✤ Church

Leader: We carry within us emotional aches of varying sorts and durations; we experience the twinges of spiritual growing pains.
People: We come in need of healing.
Leader: We endure the distresses of lingering physical ailments; we feel the torments of addictive behaviors and unresolved griefs.
People: We come in need of healing.
Leader: We know what it is like to go to pieces or to have relational bonds broken; we sense a world of hurts within an injured creation.
People: We come in need of healing.
Leader: We come to worship the God who wills us to be well, who prescribes faithfulness as a means to better health.
People: We give thanks this day for a healing faith and a loving God.

✤ Healing
✤ God, love of
✤ God, need for

Each day the sunlight or an internal clock or a bedside alarm informs us that it is time to get up.

And from that moment on, we move from time to time.

We begin with breakfast-time's three-minute egg, a bagel, a bowl of cereal, coffee on the run.

We bustle toward work so we will get there on time, or we go off to a school day where time is punctuated by bells, or we check over the day's schedule of shopping and meetings and sundry other obligations, or we measure time at home.

Then it is lunch-time, time for the soaps, time for client contacts, time for the kids to get home, dinner-time, bed-time.

For many of us there is a franticness to all of this; for others the pace is slowed by feelings of aloneness.

And what does the God we gather to worship have to say to us in the whirling midst of our minutes? Something, we believe, like this:

"Your time," says our Maker, "is my time. I created it for you. In the world that is your home, time is your living room. Use it wisely...When should it be filled with worship? All the time. When can it be our meeting place? Anytime. When will I let you know I am living there with you? Time and again, now and forever."

Welcome to worship the God of all time.

- ✤ God, presence of
- ✤ Time
- ✤ Daily life

$\mathcal{T}$he enacting of our faith is much like the making and baking, the tearing and sharing of bread.

From flour and water and leaven, the raw materials, bread comes to life. From hope and curiosity and the desire to know God, the resources, faith takes form.

The bread-to-be engages us in measuring and mixing. It requires a hands-on effort as we kneed the warmed dough and shape it. Faith likewise involves us.

Bread beckons. Its aroma reaches out as an airborne invitation to take and eat. A practiced faith also draws others with its outreach of love and its promise of nourishment for hungering spirits.

This morning we gather to worship our God, and we share together at table the Bread of Life.

- ✤ Communion
- ✤ Bread
- ✤ Faith, practice of

Leader: We travel here by car or bus or bike or train. We enter this building on foot or in a wheelchair, with the aid of a cane or in a parent's arms.

People: We come to worship in the house of God.

Leader: We arrive here alone or with members of our household or in the company of friends.

People: We come to worship as the people of God.

Leader: We identify ourselves as workers and students, job-hunters and retirees.

People: We come to worship seeking to be servants in Christ's name.
Leader: In this place and time we have a church home, a faith family, a holy purpose.
All: We come to worship with glad and grateful hearts.

✤ Faith, family of
✤ Church
✤ Worship

*W*e gather this morning in Christ's name to explore the workings of our faith, to celebrate God's active presence in our midst. In company with one another, we look to the Spirit's guidance as we strive to serve our Creator. Rejoice in the callings of our faith:
    to extend ourselves beyond kindness to compassion,
    to amplify desires for goodness into yearnings for justice,
    to stretch healthy imagination into high and holy hope,
    to deepen feelings of affection into bold and durable love.
Rejoice in the bounty of our faith. Welcome to worship.

✤ Faith, attributes of
✤ God, presence of
✤ Justice

Leader: Everything has to start sometime and somewhere and somehow...
People: Earth had its creation and we each had our day of birth.
Leader: Big oak trees had their acorn origins and beautiful flowers had their seedy beginnings.
People: The school year had its return to the classroom and this morning had its sunrise.
Leader: Everything has to start sometime and somewhere and somehow...
People: Plays with the opening of a curtain and stories with the turning of a page,
Leader: Races with a pistol's crack and dinners with a time of grace,
People: This service with our call to worship:
All: Come, let us gather together, glorifying God with praise and thanksgiving, with prayer and song!

✤ Beginnings
✤ Worship
✤ Time

Leader: When our thoughts are scattered and feelings confused and deeds undisciplined, how gracious of our God to help us order our lives.

People: We give thanks to God for calling us to discipleship.

Leader: When we sense an inner emptiness and meaning seems missing in action, how gracious of our God to open the path that leads toward true contentment.

People: We give thanks to God for calling us into mission, into service in the name of Christ.

Leader: When our attention wanders and our spirits lack focus, how gracious of our God to draw us near.

People: We give thanks to God for calling us to worship.

All: We seek to honor God in our gathering and through our serving.

✤ God, grace of
✤ Discipleship
✤ Mission

Leader: As Christian people, we are called to build human community grounded in God's love.

People: We strive to shape it. We pray for its formation. We hope to dwell within it.

Leader: Yet the things that keep us apart are legion,

People: And only the Spirit's power can draw us together. Thus, we have great hope.

Leader: We are kept apart by differences of upbringing or lifestyle or personal taste;

People: We are drawn together by the God who created us as the unique individuals we are.

Leader: We are kept apart by disagreements over political ideologies or religious practices;

People: We are drawn together by the God who alone rules the Earth, whose grandeur inspires multiple forms of service and reverent response.

Leader: We are kept apart by distinctions between races, clans and classes;

People: We are drawn together by the God whose image we all bear, whose presence in other persons we must see and feel.

Leader: We are kept apart by divisions drawn on maps or inscribed upon our hearts;

People: We are drawn together by the God who looked upon the whole of creation and pronounced it good.

All: In communion with our sisters and brothers, we come together through worshiping God.

✤ World Communion
✤ Inclusiveness
✤ Reconciliation

Leader: Between the day of our birth and the conclusion of our life in this world,

People: God nurtures and challenges us.

Leader: Between long-time friends,

People: God builds firm trust and honest understanding.

Leader: Between long-term adversaries,

People: God opens pathways to reconciliation and peace.

Leader: Between persons in need and those blessed with an abundance of resources,

People: God introduces opportunities for mutual sharing and compassionate caring.

Leader: Between brothers and sisters in Christ,

People: God fosters spirited dialogue and mutual love.

Leader: Between the ringing of our church bell and the final measures of the postlude,

People: God provides a context for worshiping together as a family of faith.

All: Thanks be to God.

✤ God, power of
✤ God, nature of
✤ Worship

Leader: By the grace of God, there is a variety of food items in the refrigerator or on the shelf, a wide selection of newspapers at the store, a vast array of things we might do with our day.

People: We give thanks to the God who provides us with choices.

Leader: By the grace of God, there are means available to improve our minds, ways to better our relationships with others, opportunities to leave the past behind and to live fully in the present.

People: We give thanks to the God who opens doors to changes.

Leader: By the grace of God, there are mysteries that struggle can help us to understand, avenues of service that beckon us to accomplish what is difficult, leaps of faith that need to be made.

People: We give thanks to the God who presents us with spiritual challenges.

All: We worship together in a family that welcomes choice and change and challenge.

✤ God, grace of
✤ Freedom
✤ Faithfulness

As we greeted one another this morning on our way to this place and as we arrived in the church building, we probably used phrases such as "hi" and "good to see you" and "what's happening" and "hello" and "how are you" and "good morning." It is likely that not one of us has yet said "good bye." After all, that is what we say when we depart, when we break contact. And yet, there is no phrase more appropriate to use when we come together, for good-bye is nothing but the shortened form of "God be with you," the best of all possible greetings.

Would it not be good if we were to start saying good-bye not just when we turned away from one another but also when we turn toward one another?

[the following may be added]

Some churches make it part of their worship service to share those words of greeting: "God be with you." Today, we are going to be one of those churches. I invite you now to share those words of welcome with your neighbors in the pews... May this be our greeting to one another always. God be with us and among us in our worship.

❖ God, presence of
❖ Greeting
❖ Church

Leader: We gather this morning to worship our ever-creative God...

People: Who formed all that is from the nothingness that was,

Leader: Who formed humankind from the stuff of this Earth and the breath of the Spirit,

People: Who formed a nation out of former slaves, wilderness wanderers, boisterous semi-believers.

Leader: We gather this morning to give thanks to our ever-creative God...

People: For sending us a Savior who took the form of a servant,

Leader: For reaching toward us with a love expressed through the forms of Word and sacrament,

People: For empowering us with a faith that takes tangible form in prayer and deed.

All: We give form to our gratitude with our presence in worship.

❖ God, as creator
❖ God, power of
❖ Gratitude

Leader: Yangtze and Danube, Congo and [name nearest river], all rivers flow toward the seas that encircle our planet.

People: May the praises of all people flow toward God as a great wave of worship.

Leader: Andes and Alps, Himalayas and [name of nearest mountains], all mountains take root in one good Earth.

People: May the hopes of all people take root in a holy love that bids us all be one.

Leader: Sirocco and zephyr, meadow breezes and [name wind characteristic to the local area], all winds move about with freedom and power.

People: May the faith of all people move about freely in the
world to empower deeds of loving kindness.

All: In the worship of this morning and the actions of every
day, may we remain always in communion with God and
with one another.

✤ World Communion
✤ Inclusiveness
✤ Environment

*I*n the congregation this morning there are eyes blinkingly
coming awake and eyes alert; there are faces familiar and faces new
to this place; there are bodies tired by work and bodies refreshed by
recreation; there are minds flashing with thoughts and minds prone
to wandering; there are worried/wearied spirits and spirits bright
with positive/potent joy...We are people with great needs and great
possibilities, and for the next few moments I invite you to look
about, not to see who is here and who is not, but rather to notice
with appreciation the presence of all who share this time. [pause]

Mark well those round about you. For they are the people you
are called to serve. They are your neighbors to love, your brothers
and sisters to nurture. They are bearers of the living Christ and min-
isters of the Holy Spirit. They are partners on the journey of faith.
When God works in wondrous and amazing ways, God works
through those whose eyes you have met, whose faces you have
observed.

Here we can begin to see the gift of one another that is God's
gift to us. Here in worshiping the one God of the world, we can
begin to sharpen a vision of one world for all God's people.
Welcome.

✤ Community
✤ Inclusiveness
✤ Faith, unity through

*T*he writer of the 133rd Psalm penned these words long ago:

"How very good and pleasant it is when kindred live together in unity! It is like the precious oil on the head, running down upon the beard, on the beard of Aaron, running down over the collar of his robes. It is like the dew of Hermon, which falls on the mountains of Zion. For there the Lord ordained his blessing, life forevermore."

The image used by the psalmist may seem strange to us, but what the writer is referring to is the custom of ancient Near Eastern hosts to welcome a guest with a lavish anointing of precious oil. It was as if to say, "Your presence and your friendship are worthy of my best." Such hearty hospitality was as natural as the falling of the dew upon the uplands of Zion.

As we gather together this morning – neighbors and friends, God's family – let us recall how good and pleasant is our unity in Christ, how strong God's blessing of life.

✤ Hospitality
✤ Unity
✤ Faith, family of

Leader: The doors of this church are closed to no one, for welcome and acceptance and understanding are the ways of our faith community.

People: We come together as open-hearted worshipers who gather to praise God.

Leader: The purpose of our common mission is to heal lives that are broken, for there are many whose sense of peace has been shattered to pieces by oppression or grief.

People: We come together as whole-hearted disciples who gather to serve in Christ's name.

Leader: The goal of our ministry is to thaw any coldness of spirit, for faith is a fire that kindles us to act with caring conviction.

People: We come together as warm-hearted people who gather to proclaim and to practice a Spirited love.

All: To the God we praise, serve and love, we offer heartfelt thanks.

✤ Faith, heart of
✤ Healing
✤ Inclusiveness

𝓗ope can be like the morning sun, rising out of deep darkness, casting it aside with a dawning light.

Hope can be like a bitter cold wind, penetrating us to the bone, rearranging portions of the world and even moving us by its power.

Hope can be like snow fresh fallen, giving a new look to the scene around us, softening its sharp edges with gentle beauty.

Hope can be like a high-flying bird, seeing far ahead beyond the horizon of creatures earthbound, moving ahead with a purposeful grace.

We gather this morning to worship our God – Creator of light and power, beauty and grace – God of hope. Welcome.

❖ God, nature of
❖ Hope
❖ Worship

Leader: We gather this morning to affirm the truth of the improbable:

People: We affirm that the Creator of all space, all time, all life, loves us individually as children and collectively as family.

Leader: We gather this morning to proclaim the implausible:

People: We proclaim that divisions of humanity – by race and clan, by economic status and political system, by physical characteristic or sexual preference – have no meaning within the community of Christ's disciples.

Leader: We gather this morning to commit ourselves to accomplishing that which seems impossible:

People: We commit ourselves to transforming this world into a place that bears the characteristics of God's realm, that reveals the nature of God's reign.

All: For this time together we offer our thanks and praise.

❖ Inclusiveness
❖ Faith, possibilities of
❖ Justice

If God were to call us to worship by means of written invitation, it might well begin with the words of a hymn:

[open envelope with invitation]

"Come, Ye Thankful People, Come!"

The gracious God almighty, Creator of heaven and earth, who gave you a home and who made you alive and able, calls you to gather together for a worship service of thanks-giving.

As reminders of the event, God will send daily reminders in the form of new days, air to breathe, bodies that function, friends who care, and feelings that move and shape you.

The God who provides everything invites you personally to share a celebration of divine grace and requests only that you bring your own gratitude.

"Come, Ye Thankful People, Come!"

✤ Thanksgiving

✤ God, grace of

✤ Gratitude

OPENING PRAYERS

Openings almost always carry a sense of drama, excitement or opportunity. Opening day at the ballpark. Opening night at the theatre. Opening moves of a chess match. Opening doors. Opening gifts. Opening minds or hearts to new understandings or relationships.

The opening prayer of a worship service is a significant liturgical event. It puts us into contact with God in a manner that is personal, forthright and direct. It puts us into contact with our brothers and sisters who share the prayer with us.

In the section of the book that follows, I offer numerous opening prayers. These may be used as written or modified to suit specific congregational circumstances. Almost all of them fit into three categories: celebration (expressions of praise to God), thanksgiving (recognitions of those things that elicit gratitude to God) or confession (acknowledgments of our need for God's forgiveness). It is my hope that every one of these prayers serves to open spirits to the power and the presence of God.

O God, you hold before us a promise. You set before us an Advent course of waiting and watching for the coming of Christ. For this, we offer our thanks.

Although your promise shines as a beckoning and guiding light, sometimes we ignore it. We turn away from its illumination and grope about in our chosen darkness. We become distracted by other lights that seem more brilliant and we find ourselves blinded by their glare. We follow the flash of bright ideas rather than rely upon the steady glow of your enduring truth.

Although the course leads Christward, we stray and wander. We succumb to temptations to go in other directions and we set ourselves on dangerous detours. We get drawn by easy paths and pleasant scenery, and we discover that the less-demanding way is a spiritual dead end.

Forgive us, we pray. Help us to hear the promise with the will to heed it. Enable us to see the course with the faith to follow it. In the name of Jesus Christ, Amen.

✤ Advent
✤ Faith, journey of
✤ Discipleship

Loving God, we enter this Advent season knowing quite a bit about light. From childhood years of falling asleep in a night-light's glow to easy-chair evenings of watching flames in a hearth, we have derived a sense of comfort and peace from many sources of brightness. Through times of travel, beacons or signals or directional devices have guided us upon our way. On countless occasions of return to our homes, we have felt welcomed by a lamp in the window or a porch light turned on, signs of our own forethought or the kindness of others. And within our yawnings at each day's dawning and our scanning the sky for evening's first star, we feel a deep gratitude for the gift of light that brings life throughout your creation.

Now, in Advent, we offer our humble thanks as we anticipate the coming of Christ, the world's true light, the provider of comfort and peace. We pray that you kindle our spirits and illuminate our minds so that our very lives become warmly welcoming to our Savior, Sovereign and Redeemer. In his name we pray. Amen.

✤ Advent
✤ Light
✤ God, guidance of

O God, Creator and Deliverer of hope, we pray that beyond the external indications of a coming Christmas, there emerge within us some holy and healthy signs of the season. Make this Advent a sacred period of enlightenment and growth, for we confess to practicing less than the fullness of faith.

Forgive us when we divert our devotion away from you and when we worship with inert spirits.

Forgive us when we assume that our faith can survive without the nourishment of study and reflection and prayer.

Forgive us when we stifle our capacity for wonder and when we insulate ourselves against your grace.

Forgive us when we neglect to give thoughtful consideration to the ways your will can be done on Earth.

Forgive us when we forget that the Messiah comes as bearer of peace and as challenger to powers that rule this world.

Free us to experience a spirited Adventure, a sensing of faith's glory. In the name of Jesus Christ, Amen.

❖ Advent
❖ Faith, components of
❖ Faith, growth of

O God, we are grateful that each year we have a time marked by wondering anticipation of our Savior's birth. Your decision to come among us as a mere baby astounds us and makes us marvel that your power and love can be so great. As we use this Advent season to prepare ourselves for the fullness of Christmas joy, help us to grow throughout its weeks. Enable us to welcome the Christchild with the excitement of the shepherds, the adoration of the Magi, the joy of Mary, the expectant hope of a waiting world. Let the light of your Spirit shine within us and through us as we worship together. In Jesus' name, Amen.

❖ Advent
❖ Joy
❖ Anticipation

Loving God, our excitement grows as days pass by this Advent season. Inspire us toward greater appreciation for the wonder of your Word made flesh, and forgive us when our attention wanders from the One who is the center of our celebration.

Inspire us toward an acceptance of your peace in our lives.

Forgive us when we cannot find it because of the pace of our lives.

Inspire us toward new understandings of the love you declare through the One who took human form and dwelt in our midst.

Forgive us when we minimize the power of your love and when we express the despair within us by placing trust in things that cannot help us.

Inspire us toward focusing our faith on acts of charity that make Christ's presence real to others.

Forgive us when we ignore Christ's presence and lose the clarity of faith that moves us to practice compassion.

Strengthen and enlighten us this Advent season. In the name of Jesus Christ we pray. Amen.

✤ Advent
✤ Faith, practice of
✤ God, presence of

O God, grant to us throughout this joyful time of year an awareness of your presence, an alertness to your Spirit's movement, an appreciation for your creative love.

May the table treats of this season, the cider and stollen and cookies and cocoa, increase our thankfulness for the Earth's bounty.

May the decorations that adorn our homes, window candles and colored lights, evergreen garlands and grapevine wreaths, bear witness to the gladness we feel at Christ's birth.

May the exchange of holiday greetings, by card and phone and letter and email and fax, encourage us to extend the reach of our faith community.

May the giving that characterizes Christmas—checks for charities and presents for friends, mailed packages and hand-delivered parcels—signify the true generosity of our spirits.

May the abundance of love, voiced in carols and embodied in embraces, revealed in scriptures and acknowledged in prayer, increase ever more as we live out our faith. In the name of Jesus Christ, Amen.

✤ Advent
✤ God, presence of
✤ Faith, symbols of

O God, we are thankful that you chose to make yourself known to us as a Person.

You have become present to us in a way we can understand. Forgive us when we do not understand.

When we are shocked and surprised by the wonder of your love, we may not know just how to respond.

When we feel awkward or unworthy at having your Child in our midst, we may seem less than grateful.

When we are beckoned by Jesus to follow him in order to find ourselves, we may feel our sense of identity threatened.

Help us in this Advent time to make room for Christ not at an inn but within ourselves.

Give us the clear vision that sees the great things you have done; fill us with the eagerness to come running at your call.

Grant us the ability to recognize your presence in the ordinary and commonplace; build within us the wisdom to worship when we find you there.

O God, light up our Advent with your love. Infuse this time of worship with joy and peace. Amen.

✤ Advent
✤ Common life
✤ God, love of

O God, on this night of miracle and wonder, give us the wisdom to realize that with the birth of Jesus we, too, are born to new life. Help us to see that the world is changed by your presence within it; its powers of selfishness, death and darkness are broken by Jesus Christ, born a Child at once gentle and strong, who came to give life and light. Remind us that your power does not fade with the notes of the last carol or drop off like needles from a browning tree, nor can it be packed away like ornaments in forgettable attic places of our lives. We are grateful that your power is constant and lives as the Child lives, growing and glowing within us. So may our celebrations be powerful, full of hearty feelings of love, peace, joy, and wonder. We thank you, O God, for the Christmas gift of yourself. Amen.

✤ Advent
✤ God, presence of
✤ Incarnation

Loving God, we thank you for arriving among us as a Child. Throughout the coming new year, help us to see our hopes as the children of our spirits. And give us the patience to devote steadfast prayerful attention to them.

We hope for the peace of Christ.

We hope for the justice he sought.

We hope for the joy he promised.

We hope of the love he practiced.

As the Christchild goes with us and grows within us, we believe that our hopes will be nurtured and nourished, that the world can be changed by their realization.

We experience our Christ as an immediate, indwelling, inspiring presence that draws us together for worship and service. Amen.

❖ Advent

❖ Hope

❖ Incarnation

O God, we give thanks this day for the colors and tones of the Advent season, for the tapestry of joyful feelings they combine to create.

Accept our gratitude, we pray,

For the red of holly berries and of faces fire-warmed after hours of sledding,

For the green of front door wreaths and of living room trees,

For the darkness of a holy night and a stable birthing place,

For the brightness of a guiding star and a divine promise fulfilled.

For the golden ring of angel voices and the golden hope for peace on Earth.

Grant us appreciation in this time of preparation; fill us with joy as we anticipate the coming of the Christ. Amen.

❖ Advent

❖ Colors

❖ Incarnation

God of all the years, God of all persons upon the Earth, we couple our praise with our prayer, for it is with confidence in your forgiveness that we make our honest confession.

We have been more adept at professing our faith than at practicing it. Although we place ourselves in the ranks of believers and acknowledge your indwelling presence, we often refrain from letting your Spirit be our guidance system. We balk at doing the very things Jesus commended and commanded: praying for enemies, working for justice, giving unselfishly, loving unconditionally, healing hurts, trusting you. Sometimes, when our faith is weak, we succumb to the temptation of regarding these things as optional rather than essential. Forgive us when we excuse our inaction. And fill us, we ask, with the energy and the wisdom to respond to Jesus' teachings with daily dedication. We seek to develop our faith through its practice.

Age upon age, your people have relentlessly tried your patience and defied your will. We have done so ourselves. Yet in this our confession, we feel the renewal of forgiveness and we sense the freeing power of your grace. So it is with unburdened spirits that we close our prayer, offering it in the name of Jesus Christ. Amen.

✣ New Year
✣ Faith, essentials of
✣ Grace

Loving God, Creator of all that is, we ask for the strength and wisdom to acknowledge that you are the Author of our lives, the sole authority that can lead us consistently in the ways of truth and love. Through our deeds, speak your Word to the world; through our prayers, attune us to the guiding voice of your Holy Spirit.

We confess that we have succumbed to temptations. We have exalted our own desires and minimized the demands of discipleship. We have measured our success more by acquisitions than by commitments. We have defined neighbor in terms more restrictive than those used by Jesus. We have reneged on promises initially made in good faith. We have neglected to nurture the kind of curiosity essential to the maturing of belief. Forgive us, we pray.

By your grace, renew us. With your compassion, equip us. Through your love, empower us. In the name of Jesus Christ we pray. Amen.

✣ Forgiveness
✣ God, authority of
✣ Discipleship

Gracious God, we realize that you invite us to talk with you at any time and in any place. We deeply appreciate the freedom of access you grant us and recognize it as a firm indicator of your care. We appreciate, too, the occasions when we can compose ourselves in the postures of prayer taught us in early childhood. During the Lenten season, alert us to meanings that emerge through the very manner of our praying, through the bowing of heads, through the closing of eyes, through the clasping or upraising of hands.

We bow our heads to acknowledge your greatness, to show humble reverence.

We close our eyes to remind ourselves to look at things from your perspective, to put aside an insistence on our own fallible views.

We clasp our hands to signify your power to unite, to make diversity more a cause for celebration than for conflict.

We upraise our hands to open ourselves to blessings received.

Grant us the individual and the corporate wisdom to pray with honesty, care and conviction. And though you do not always respond in the ways we desire, we pray that you keep us steadfastly reliant upon your grace. We are grateful that you love us and that you guide us toward what is best for us. Transform our gratitude into faithful discipleship. In the name of Jesus Christ, Amen.

✤ Lent
✤ Prayer, practice of
✤ Discipleship

O God, we unite in prayer readily and gladly even as we acknowledge the diversity of our spiritual needs and longings.

Some of us come grief-stricken or downcast; others of us come in an attitude of celebration.

Some of us face difficult decisions and uncertainties; others of us face the excitement of newly chosen challenge.

Some of us seek the relief of accepting forgiveness; others of us seek a release from the bonds of bitterness toward others.

Some of us feel burdened by disability or disease; others of us feel keen appreciation for the good health we enjoy.

Some of us sense a numbing despair at the problems in our world; others of us sense great opportunities for enacting our faith.

No matter what the state of our spirits, we share, almighty God, a common need for your gracious guidance and sustaining love. With voices united, we pray in Jesus' name. Amen.

❖ Lent
❖ Faith, practice of
❖ Diversity

Loving God, you graciously provide us with opportunities for worship, and these serve as paths of entrance into the realm of faithful living.

Help us, we pray, to get into the practice of worshiping regularly in ways that strengthen us for accomplishing the tasks of discipleship.

Speak to us through the silence of reflection, the wisdom of your Word, the mystery of sacrament, the conversation of prayer.

Grant us an appreciation for worshipful events in our everyday lives, moments of wondrous incarnations and deep insights.

Teach us to recognize the Spirit at work in the actions of those who render kindness to the dejected, those who exercise compassion toward the ill or broken-hearted, those who reach out to embrace the forsaken, those who seek justice for the oppressed or abused.

Show us your way, O God, and allow us to walk it in companionship with the Christ in whose name we pray. Amen.

❖ Lent
❖ Faith, journey of
❖ Faith, components of

Loving God, as we look ahead to the season of Lent, a period for devoting attention to improving our spiritual health and fitness, grant us the courage to acknowledge the ways in which our faith is out of shape.

We confess that our spirits have not been fed upon the most wholesome foods. We have snacked upon pettiness, swallowed untruths, savored opportunities to judge others.

We confess that our deepest beliefs have suffered from lack of exercise. We have been more lethargic than energetic in the practice of Christly compassion, and sometimes our attempts to reach out to neighbors reveal a love more stiff than limber.

We confess that our endurance in matters of faith has not fully been developed. We have been lax in training ourselves spiritually, and we have found ourselves more exhausted than strengthened by choosing to pursue our culture's pace instead of your peace.

Forgive us, we ask. Guide us, we pray. In the name of Jesus Christ, Amen.

✤ Lent
✤ Faith, development of
✤ Fitness, spiritual

O God, whenever we greet one another and gather together in your name, may it be with a full sense of your presence, with a deep appreciation for your guiding power. We ask that you build in us an experience and an understanding of the church as a place of stories…a place for hearing stories, for sharing stories, for enacting stories.

Sharpen our ability to listen to the accounts of biblical people, to participate in their struggles, trials and triumphs. Help us to hear in such a way that we are able to discern your call for faithfulness within the arena of human history. Attune our ears to the gospel of Jesus Christ, the greatest story ever told.

Encourage us to share our life stories with one another, to open ourselves so the Spirit may reveal new possibilities for reconciliation and growth, intimacy and joy. You have created us for companionship in Christ. As his life story touches us, draw us together.

Grant us the energy and the will to enact the beliefs that are revealed through the accounts of prophets and gospel writers and authors of letters, through the stories of brothers and sisters in the faith. We acknowledge that only through our words and deeds will the story continue to come to life.

Forgive us, O God, when we are poor listeners, when we are hesitant sharers, when we are timid enacters. Speak your story to us throughout our worship, and may our lives reflect its power.

In the name of Jesus Christ, Amen.

✤ Stories
✤ Faith, activity/activities of
✤ Church

O God, through Jesus Christ you have invited all who are heavy-laden to come to you for rest, and you have asked us to take up your yoke. Give us the wisdom and the strength of spirit to do so. Help us to realize that the point of accepting that yoke is to get us to lay down our own burdens.

What you place upon us, loving God, is as light as you promised, and yet it is also substantial in ways that build our spirits...

You place upon us the weight of obedience. May our obedience be as a ship's anchor that plumbs to the depths; let it keep our faith from drifting in stormy times.

You place upon us the weight of discipline. May our discipline be as a ship's ballast that gives stability; let it serve to keep our faith upright and on course.

And you place upon us the weight of love. May our love be as a ship's cargo that fills the emptiness within; let it be what we carry abroad and what we do not hold to ourselves.

Accept the burdens we place before you and enable us to take your yoke upon us, for we trust and know that you are forgiving and giving. In Jesus' name we pray. Amen.

✤ Burdens
✤ Yoke
✤ Faith, characteristics of

O God of strength, we thank you for giving us cause to celebrate on this day of palms, for today we remember that Jesus risked himself for his brothers and sisters...for us. Give us the strength and resolution to follow his example. Enter among us, we pray:

✛ with compassion, for those who bear physical pains or grief;
✛ with joy, for persons who stand in need of encouragement and hope;
✛ with peace, for families in conflict and neighbors at war;
✛ with decisiveness, for those who struggle with uncertainty or wavering spirits.

Help us, God, to be persons who can enter your Realm as followers of Jesus Christ. In his name we pray. Amen.

❖ Palm Sunday
❖ Faith, strength of
❖ Discipleship

Gracious God, we give thanks for your presence among us as we gather to worship this evening. Help us to come to new understandings of your love, and grant us insights as we strive to focus on the rejections and abuses endured by Jesus. Although it sometimes seems to our ways of thinking that you have abandoned us to the forces of darkness, as it appeared that you had abandoned Jesus, we ask that you affirm in our lives the power that is never absent, however little we perceive it, however often we ignore it. We pray in the name of Jesus, despised and rejected and yet called Savior. And we pray in the words he taught us, saying... [the prayer of Jesus]

❖ Maundy Thursday
❖ God, presence of
❖ God, power of

Good and gracious God,
If our minds have ever succumbed to dark thoughts,
If our hearts have sunk into the depths of despair,
If our spirits have wearied of empty promises,
We rejoice this day!
In our minds, bright hopes arise,
In our hearts, love soars to new heights,
In our spirits, we sense that an empty tomb is a promise
    fulfilled.
For new life given through the risen Christ, we offer our
    thanks and praise.
Amen.

❖ Easter
❖ God, praise to
❖ Joy

Gracious God, we were less than perfect last week in showing our concern for your world and its inhabitants. We consumed more than we needed, refrained from acts of charity, neglected to pray fervently for victims of conflict.

Gracious God, we were less than perfect last week in building sound relationships with others. We backed away from opportunities for reconciliation, made judgments self-serving or harsh, refused to identify with the feelings of persons we cherish.

Gracious God, we were less than perfect last week in taking care of ourselves. We wasted time or energies, did things that harmed our health, devoted little effort to improving our spiritual well-being.

This morning, as we start a new week, we come to you in prayer knowing that through your forgiveness of our failings, we begin to understand our potential for goodness. Hold before us the perfect example of Jesus Christ, whose humanity instructs us in the ways of faithfulness, whose sovereignty in our lives gives us the courage to follow where he leads.

In his name we pray. Amen.

- ✤ Forgiveness
- ✤ God, love of
- ✤ Faithfulness

O God, we gather together this morning as a circle of friends within the greater circle of faith. We are especially grateful that you embrace us with your love and power, for as our lives come full circle, it is only as we trust in these that laughter can truly fill all our days.

It is no small gift to experience your grace in the enjoyment of our lifetimes. For these things we give thanks:

- ✚ for the gummy giggles of grinning babies;
- ✚ for the playful chuckles of children;
- ✚ for the rowdy, rambunctious humor of adolescents;
- ✚ for the mature and pointed wit of adults;
- ✚ for the appreciative laughter of elders.

As we grow in the faith, through recognition of your past support and future promise, may the circle of friends, the circle of laughter, expand and remain forever unbroken. We ask that your bright Spirit fill our worship with fitting praise. In the name of Jesus Christ, Amen.

❖ Faith, circle of
❖ Laughter
❖ Faith, development of

O God, Creator of our freedom, we are drawn to worship as a fitting response to your love for us. As we have come here by choice, we have also come to receive your challenge. In our time of worship, hold before us the teachings of Jesus Christ so that they claim us with a gentle power. Remind us how our commitment to Christ integrates worship with the deeds of every day; here we confess our weaknesses, discover our strengths, and offer ourselves in service to a world that is both our home and your creation.

Empower us to love one another with the unselfishness Jesus showed and shared.

Encourage us to accept the challenge of reaching toward our own full potentials.

Enable us to confront oppression and hostility with a gospel of justice and peace.

Be with us always in Spirit and in truth, through Jesus Christ. Amen.

❖ Worship
❖ Faith, activity/activities of
❖ God, love of

Loving God, Parent of all humankind, you created us to inhabit your world, to dwell together as family, to worship you in word and deed.

We confess to inequities in humanity's living arrangements. While some reside in splendor, others sleep in streets. While some install security systems, others cannot escape the terrible violence and insecurity that surrounds them. We acknowledge injustices, and we admit as well that our planetary housekeeping has been so shoddy it endangers us all. Forgive us, we pray.

We confess to actions that fragment the family or that cause it stress. Sometimes, in our dealings with one another, we let ethnic or racial or religious differences blind us to our essential unity. Often we practice unconcern or coercion more ably than we do caring or acceptance. Forgive us, we pray.

We confess to neglecting our spiritual health and to avoiding participation in forms of service that our faith commends. Our attention to your Word and will has been deficient. Forgive us, we pray.

Help us to become better Earth keepers, more compassionate members of the human family, more dedicated people of faith. In the name of Jesus Christ, Amen.

✤ Forgiveness
✤ Justice
✤ Unity

O God, in this season of warming winds, we offer thanks that you hold us as a kite master holds a kite.

We are grateful that your grasp is firm and yet not too tight; we feel our connectedness to you and know that you will not lose grip even when the winds change, when life's updrafts and down-currents toss us about. Your hand serves to guide us gently; you do not rip us harshly through winds that can tear us apart. Instead, you hold us with gentle steadfastness so our spirits can soar.

We are grateful, God, that you keep the line that binds us to you from becoming too slack. We are not set adrift to battle the buffeting currents and crosswinds, and we know that without some tautness to the line we would readily crash. Your loving hand pulls us toward you, and when that happens, our spirits stretch and we fly to new heights in our faith.

The winds of your Spirit blow warm and strong. Help us to ride upon them with grace. In the name of Jesus Christ, Amen.

✤ Seasons, spring
✤ Faith, freedom of
✤ God, hand of

Creating and uniting God, you have drawn us together into this church; you have granted us keen perceptions of needs to address; you have redeemed and renewed us; you have set us apart to do your will in the world. Thank you.

Thank you for transforming strangers into friends, for giving us one another as trusted co-workers within the faith community.

Thank you for turning us toward persons who are estranged or neglected or oppressed, for urging us to practice compassion as a way of life.

Thank you for teaching us values that seem strange in the context of our culture, for reminding us through scripture and experience of love's awesome power.

Whenever we gather, we feel gratitude for the opportunity to share ministry and to express our faith through word and deed. We pray in the name of our Savior, Jesus Christ. Amen.

- ❖ Church
- ❖ Church, annual meeting
- ❖ Faith, outreach of

O God, when Jesus ministered among us in the realm of human history, he accurately and affectionately called you "Abba." Through all his words and actions, he shared his knowledge of you, deepened our understanding of your will, drew us into the intimacy of a holy contact called prayer. He expanded family boundaries and informed us that we, by invitation and by grace, are your children of promise.

We confess, however, that even when your guidance is clear, we stray from the right path and exercise our freedom of disobedience. We are more quarrelsome than compassionate, more self-protective than honest, more close-minded than open-hearted, more judgmental than just, more controlling than loving. We make our choices and find ourselves lost.

Gracious and mighty God, forgive us. We humbly acknowledge that only when we accept your active parenting of humankind can we trust in having a future abounding with hope. Turn us. Teach us. Embrace us. Empower us. These things we ask in the name of your Child, Jesus Christ. Amen.

- ❖ God, parenthood of
- ❖ Faith, journey
- ❖ Grace

O God, we have come gladly this day to worship you with spoken words and songs. We confess that we bring with us many "ought-to-have-dones" we have neglected, many "ought-not-to-have-dones" we have accomplished. Forgive our failings and frailties. Enable us to discover moments of holy laughter in our lives and to recognize through them the surprising power of your grace.

Charge us to be bearers of light and life. Teach us to be jesters who challenge worldly powers with lively words of truth. Grant us the courage to follow a daring Christ who saves us from any somber hopelessness. As you move among us and within us during this time of worship, fill us with joy as your Spirit enters in. In the name of our Liberator and Redeemer, Jesus Christ, Amen.

❖ Forgiveness
❖ Joy
❖ Faithfulness

Gracious God, we confess before you and in the company of one another that we fall short of living the fullness of our faith. We parcel out our love for you and for our neighbors as though you do not require us to offer it entirely and gladly. Forgive, we pray, a fragmentary devotion.

Our minds have moved away from attentiveness to your will, and only occasionally do we focus on what you would have us do in the situations of daily life. We are more concerned with what others think than what you desire.

Our eyes have grown blind to certain injustices or societal pains, and the tears that can prompt action seldom fall. We prefer to keep out of sight the very things that develop a depth of compassion.

Our hands have become more grasping than giving, and we assert ourselves by possessing more than we need or by withholding much of what we can offer to others. We retain more readily than we release.

Our feet have wandered from paths of righteousness and service, and our spirits have strayed off course. We walk through our days without clarity of purpose.

Loving God, forgive us. Renew our minds, make clear our eyes, use our hands, and direct our feet. We seek to follow the Christ in whose name we pray. Amen.

❖ Faith, activity/activities of
❖ God, devotion to
❖ Forgiveness

Loving God, as we speak this prayer, we know that you listen to the concerns we express, that you hear even those needs and hopes spoken only by a silent voice within us. We are confident, too, that when we listen for your Word, you will speak in ways which comfort and encourage, correct and empower, challenge and guide. In this opening prayer of our worship service, we ask that you open us to experiences of bolder discipleship and deeper faithfulness.

Befriend us daily through the companionship of Jesus who is Sovereign over our common life.

Stretch us from parochial interests toward true neighborliness with all who share this Earth.

Counsel us in times when hurt or despair close us in.

Redirect us when we fail to reach out to others or do so with self-serving intent.

Motivate us to take on the holy tasks of spreading love and practicing hospitality.

Forgive us when our spirits weary, when our devotion lapses, when our willfulness impedes your work, when our hearts or minds close themselves to you.

We pray that our attentiveness increases so we may always be in communion with Jesus Christ, our Teacher, Redeemer and Friend. Amen.

✤ Faithfulness
✤ Discipleship
✤ Faith, activity/activities of

O God, we gather this morning as your children. We pray that in our worship and in our continued maturing into greater faithfulness you keep alive within us the best of what is childlike.

When we confront what is new or gain fresh insights into the everyday, preserve in us a sense of wonder.

As we strive toward understanding your majesty or toward coming to grips with the expanse and inclusiveness of your realm, preserve our capacity for awe.

Through times and situations that tempt us to be rigid or to reject the input of others, preserve a pliability in our thinking.

In moments when animosity impedes our capacity to love or when our relationship with you seems less than personal, preserve our simple affections.

And God, amidst the minor chaos of daily life or the feelings of helplessness in a world careening out of control, preserve in us the joy of imagining a new world to live in, even a world that can be called your Realm.

Hear our prayer as a psalm of hope, offered in the name of Jesus Christ. Amen.

✤ Hope
✤ Faith, childlike
✤ Common life

Loving God, you bid us be all we can be and you accept us as we are. We pray that by your grace and power, those things that are stumbling blocks to our spiritual growth may be overcome. Show us the way in this time of worship. Teach us through the events of our lives.

When our capacity to sin binds us with tension, enable us to relax by trusting in your forgiveness.

When our situation is one of peril or distress, enable us to discover in your love the resource of restoration.

When our frailties get us down and keep us there, enable us to laugh at ourselves by relying on your strength.

When our tendency to become burdened by work makes us anxious, enable us to play by responding to your invitation to participate freely in the game of grace and the joys of life.

Lead us, we pray, in the ways of Jesus Christ. Amen.

✤ Grace
✤ God, reliance on
✤ Common life

O God, within the broad expanse of prayer, we speak in a way we speak nowhere else; within the sacred space of prayer, we listen in a way we listen nowhere else; within the intimate confines of prayer, we meet you as we meet you nowhere else. Help us to become practiced in prayer, to exercise the freedom and discipline it requires.

Hold us to absolute honesty in our speaking, whether we are describing our innermost thoughts or relating our concern for persons in distant regions of the world. May our language be that of integrity and compassion.

Enable our listening to be keen, whether we are attempting to hear the whispers of your Spirit or striving to follow the clear call that bids us enact your just love. May our hearing be attuned to your will and Word.

Draw us near as we meet with you in prayer, whether we are struggling to balance our neediness with a fear of closeness or yearning to open ourselves entirely to you. May our approach be marked by passion and reverence.

For the privilege of prayer and for the opportunities of service, we give our thanks. In Jesus' name, Amen.

❖ Prayer, practice of
❖ Prayer, characteristics of
❖ God, listening for

O God, we come to you as persons striving to know better what it means to live our faith. Increase our knowledge. Teach us.

We thank you for providing us over time with so much spiritual guidance: the words of scripture, the ways of Jesus, the traditions of the church, the witness of faithful men and women through the ages, the guidings of the Spirit. We have taken in a great deal and our beliefs have taken shape. Yet we confess, loving God, that often we have been slothful or cowardly in applying what we have learned. Our faith has remained more in the form of intention than practice. Forgive us, and enable us truly to be educated by having the best within us, your very image, drawn out and revealed.

Help us to develop among us a common sense of your will and a common sensitivity to the needs of all others in your creation. Grant us a trust in the capacity to grow spiritually, and fill us with diligence and commitment directed toward study of our faith.

Open our minds and hearts; enter in as we open this time of worship. We pray in the name of Jesus Christ. Amen.

❖ Christian education
❖ Faith, growth of
❖ Discipleship

Almighty and merciful God, we approach you in prayer acknowledging that you know us better than we know ourselves, confessing that our faith journey is marked by aimless meanderings and dangerous detours, trusting that your forgiveness can get us on course. We note especially that the very things we reject are often gifts you have provided to help us make good spiritual progress.

Forgive us for rejecting the gifts you offer to us...the resolve that motivates work for peace and justice, the courage that Jesus can instill in those who dare his loving ways, the serenity that derives from prayer, the hope that never relents.

Forgive us for rejecting the gifts of others...the wisdom of persons we label as backward, the perspective of those "not like us," the petitions of those in need, the healthy and holy insights of critics and fools and prophets.

Forgive us for rejecting the gifts within ourselves...the talents we hide or set aside, the valuable experiences we hesitate to share, the spiritual instincts we ignore or neglect to develop, the untapped potential for joyful service in Christ's name.

As we ask your forgiveness, we anticipate your renewing activity in our lives, and so we pray with confidence and gratitude. In Jesus' name, Amen.

✤ Forgiveness
✤ Faith, attentiveness to
✤ Gifts

Loving God, we strive to be people who live faithfully, who serve gladly, who remember you regularly, who love others unconditionally. Yet we also acknowledge that our faithfulness has been impaired by inner conflicts or lack of courage, that our spiritual effectiveness has been limited by concessions to stubborn selfishness or indifference to the needs of others. We confess our failings and we affirm our desire to experience faith as vital and active.

Forgive us...

When our hot-headedness causes rancor instead of reconciliation, when our cold-heartedness causes compassion to shrink.

Forgive us...

When rough times turn us away rather than toward a firm trust in you, when smooth words from our lips mask impure intentions.

Forgive us...

When hard decisions get made without taking your will into account, when soft commitments to you stunt our spiritual growth.

We rely on your mercy and grace, and we gratefully receive your forgiveness as offered through Jesus Christ. We pray in his name. Amen.

✤ Faithfulness
✤ Forgiveness
✤ Discipleship

Loving God, we long to be whole and healthy persons, to dwell daily in a state of well-being, to act in ways that create a more holy and wholesome world.

Grant us the measure of courage necessary to overcome unhealthy habits, those that harm our own bodies or endanger the lives of others.

Help us to develop healthy attitudes that are positive in outlook, that enable us to form solutions rather than to place blame, that respect the dignity of all.

Enable us to envision a future that is a picture of health for humankind, and provide us with the spiritual energy to create such a future. So may your will be done on Earth.

We pray in the name of Jesus Christ. Amen.

✤ Healing
✤ Faith, gifts of
✤ Wholeness

Eternal God, you have provided as our dwelling place a wondrous creation and a span of time. Teach us to regard the Earth as a living body requiring our tender care. And help us to learn through worship and service a manner of inhabiting time that is in accord with your will.

Remind us again and again of the psalmist's proclamation: "This is the day our God has made; let us rejoice and be glad in it." May those words inspire joyfulness and build within us deep appreciation for the abiding love that moves you to create each new day as a gift to us.

Grant us the wisdom to see that the fullness of time is not a burden so long as it is filled with your grace rather than with our expectations, our demands, our sometimes selfish strivings.

Develop in us the maturity of spirit that will enable us to withdraw from our continual struggles with time which will allow us to cease contending with it and so discover a welcome serenity and a restorative peace.

During this time of worship as a community of faith, instill in us a sense of reverence that we can carry with us when we leave this place. Help us, O God, to feel the holiness of every moment. In the name of Jesus Christ we pray. Amen.

✤ Time
✤ Faithfulness
✤ Faith, practice of

Gracious God, we give thanks for the persistence of your presence...

✟ you forgive us when we imagine that to be impossible;
✟ you enter our lives in ways that we consider implausible;
✟ you comfort us in times of tension, trial and turmoil;
✟ you join us in our joys and encourage our fulfillment;
✟ you call forth our best while loving us without condition;
✟ you heal our hurts and restore our souls.

We thank you with all our hearts and offer our prayer in Jesus' name. Amen.

✤ God, presence of
✤ Grace
✤ Gratitude

Loving and sustaining God, Sovereign through all eternity, we offer this prayer with humble hearts. We confess to living more as tourists than as full-time residents of your Realm.

We have made numerous excursions while refraining from settling down into commitments of community.

We have often shopped around for spiritual bargains at the expense of passing by a quality and enduring faith.

We have sometimes regarded the problems or needs of others as rain upon our vacation, and in our resentment we have valued contentment above compassion.

Forgive us. Help us to become dwellers in your Realm. Root us in faithfulness and grant us depth of belief. In the name of Jesus Christ, Amen.

✤ Faith, journey of
✤ Discipleship
✤ Faith, practice of

O God, grant us the courage to follow Christ and the willingness to receive the Spirit's guidance. Preserve us from arrogance of belief but help us maintain the integrity of humble discipleship.

We confess to being lax or hesitant in the expression of our commitment to you.

We are slow to sing the full song of faith with its lively harmony and rhythm, its melody of loving-kindness and refrain of justice.

We are content to say the expected and acceptable while avoiding sharp statements of truth that give voice to the Spirit's power.

We are reluctant to look at our world with the eyes of Christ, to see clearly its pains and wrongs, to envision better ways.

Forgive us, we pray. Strengthen us with the resolve to distinguish ourselves through service and to profess our faith through obedience. In the name of Jesus Christ, Amen.

✤ Music
✤ Faith, activity/activities of
✤ Faithfulness

Gracious and caring God, no matter what our age, we are all still trying to grow as Christians, to become wiser and more mature people of faith.

We confess that often what we do, say, or think is not as kind or loving as it can be.

Sometimes we hurt other people by ignoring them and sometimes we hurt them with actions that are mean-spirited.

Occasionally we give in to greed or succumb to selfishness or hold on to hatreds.

Now and then we find ourselves being naughty when we know better and being disrespectful of those who can direct us toward what is right.

We seek your help and forgiveness, O God, for we want to grow in faith, to know the joys of healthy community and deep belief. In Jesus' name we pray. Amen.

+ Faith, growth of
+ Forgiveness
+ Discipleship

Gracious God, we come to you in prayer confessing our need of your mercy and power, professing our confidence in your forgiveness and love.

We look at your beloved creation and see its wholeness shattered by abuse and misuse and neglect; we have treated the Earth's resources as conveniences available to support our lifestyle rather than as gifts offered to sustain our spirits.

We look at the fragmented human family and note the disintegration of nations and the upheaval of lives; we have not yet learned to let go of animosities or to resolve problems without resorting to violence.

We look at ourselves and acknowledge the difficulty we sometimes have in holding all the pieces together; we have relied upon the wisdom of this world and convinced ourselves that solace and meaning can be found apart from faith.

Now we look toward you, Source of our being, Parent to all humankind, Teacher and Redeemer. We pray that your Spirit dwell in our midst so that we live in companionship with creation, in familial relationship with our sisters and brothers, in peace with ourselves. By your grace and power, transform us. In Jesus' name, Amen.

+ Environment
+ Faith, practice of
+ God, power of

O God, Creator of this Earth and Lover of all humankind, we offer thanks for the patience of your love and the constancy of your grace. On this World Communion Sunday, we confess to insensitivities of spirit. We have not savored each new day. We have not seen injustices right before our eyes. We have withheld touches that can heal. We have closed our ears to cries of pain. And yet we are yours, and in this we find our hope. By your grace, may we flavor the world with good news, look toward a peace-filled future, extend ourselves for the sake of others, and listen to hear what hurts. We pray in the name of Jesus Christ. Amen.

❖ World Communion
❖ Grace
❖ Justice

O God, giver of life, breath of Spirit, be our inspiration through every day. Help us to be lovers of your ways, followers of your Son, bearers of liberating Good News to our neighbors. Give us the strength and the courage to exemplify faithfulness, to live for you in a world that seems often to be so much against you.

Forgive us when we ignore or neglect you, when we perceive dimly and appreciate inadequately the steadfastness of your love. Forgive us when our indecision or apathy hinders your Spirit's work. Forgive us when we get so set in our ways that we close ourselves off to what you would reveal. Forgive us when we have so much faith in our doubts that you can only doubt our desire to be faithful.

Help us always, gracious God, toward a vital faith, toward a discipleship that is professed through the quality of our deeds and the style of our life. May the Spirit poured out in baptism flow freely among us. Renew us as your people; make us whole and holy. In the name of Jesus Christ, Amen.

❖ Baptism
❖ Faithfulness
❖ Grace

Creative and powerful God, though we strive to grow in faith, we struggle to come clean before you. We falsely assume that by keeping unacknowledged our darker side, our impure motives and our well-concealed faults, we somehow hide ourselves from your view. Forgive us for trying to avoid the light of your love, for by so doing we have evaded the embrace of your forgiveness.

We pray that you forgive us when we get entrenched in patterns of behavior that allow us to neglect you, when we become entranced by ways that ignore your will.

Forgive us when we treat others in a manner that demeans them, when we set aside those aspects of your love that demand the most of our faith.

Forgive us when we show little respect for your call to discipleship, when we do little to convey the power of your love, grace and compassion to our brothers and sisters.

Hear our prayer offered in Jesus' name. Amen.

✤ Forgiveness
✤ Faith, honesty of
✤ Justice

O God, our Creator and Sustainer, help us develop into good stewards of all that you entrust to us. Enable us to recognize our giftedness and to receive with gratitude our faith's treasures.

Grant us full awareness of the treasure of your presence. Let us come to understand how the continuing story of faith has currency and worth for us, even as it gets told through our very lives.

Grant us honest acceptance of the treasure of your grace. Let us realize how our faith is nourished and nurtured by that which you freely give to us, an amazing grace we can neither earn nor control.

Grant us hearty appreciation for the treasure of your love. Let us acknowledge, in truth and in faith, how love grows not by accumulating it but by giving it away.

As persons who treasure the opportunity to be servants and stewards in Christ's name, we offer this prayer in reverent gratitude. Amen.

✤ Stewardship
✤ Faith, treasures of
✤ Gratitude

Loving God, when we take a careful and caring look around us, we feel serious concern over what the future holds. We see international tensions and intra-familial conflicts; we observe disregard of human dignity and disrespect for basic values; we take note of ecological negligence and economic uncertainty. We see that our culture makes it far easier to be a consumer than a conserver, a predator than a prophet, a blamer than a healer. We cast our eyes roundabout and wonder where it will all end up.

Help us, we pray, to look to the future with a clear understanding of where it all began. This world took shape as the product of your creative love. You proclaimed it good and blessed it with your presence.

We confess that disregard of your will and your ways has imperiled us. And we acknowledge that when we turn to you with humble trust, restoration and renewal start. By your grace and with our active commitment, the future can be bright with promise. In the name of Jesus Christ we offer this prayer and anticipate new beginnings. Amen.

❖ Future
❖ Hope
❖ Justice

Gracious God, we pray that by the power of your Spirit working within us our faith takes form. Shape it according to your will so it has the strength of truth, the structural integrity of justice, the beauty of steadfast love.

We ask that our faith be constantly reformed by the interaction of prayer and practice, by the creative contact between abiding Word and new situations. Help us to mature in spirit as we apply our beliefs to our behavior.

We confess that our faith needs to be informed by greater attentiveness to scripture, greater dedication to sharing the good news of your love. Grant us an outlook on life that is spiritually acute and clear.

We voice a firm hope that our faith becomes the source of transformation in our lives. Let it be the establisher of values, the mediator of relationships, the enabler of growth.

Hear our prayer offered in the name of Jesus Christ. Amen.

❖ Reformation Sunday
❖ Faith, growth of
❖ Faith, form of

O God, you have given us things visible and invisible...

✢ a wondrously colorful natural world, an unseen forgiveness.
You have given us understandings spoken and unspoken...

✢ the crisp parables, the silent answering of prayers.
You have given us peak experiences and common occur-
rences...

✢ new births of babies and everyday renewals of friendships.

So much you have given already, yet as we enter worship, we do not
hesitate to ask for this one more thing: give to us, loving God, the
gratitude within our hearts that turns deep appreciation into genuine praise. In the name of Jesus Christ, for whom we are ever-
thankful, Amen.

✤ Thanksgiving
✤ God, generosity of
✤ Gratitude

Words of assurance

*T*he words of assurance offered after a prayer serve to remind us of how God hears us and responds to us...with attentiveness and compassion, with forgiveness and grace. The simple and brief sentences are meant to convey something profound and extensive. The news does not get much better than this: God attends to our needs, God addresses them with compassionate care, God forgives relentlessly, God exults in practicing an amazing grace.

When we are "Home on the Range," it may be that "seldom is heard a discouraging word," but in the course of daily life, discouraging words creep in with numbing regularity. We hear them at times from friends or partners or business associates or acquaintances. We catch them in the headlines and on newscasts. The one place that discouraging words have no place is in Christ's church. We are emphatically a resurrection/good news people who claim a gallows – the cross – as our central symbol of hope. Our faith affirms in a steadfastly encouraging manner that God overcomes death with life, transforms despair into promise, replaces oppression with justice, and greets confession with forgiveness. What could be more reassuring? In all these ways we receive the love of God.

A point of information: The words of assurance offered in this section of the book are intended for general use throughout the church year. When a particular piece is specific to a holiday or occasion, it is noted.

Our God seeks to brighten our lives with holy presence, to enlighten us in ways that lead to growth of faith and extension of service. This Advent season, we receive the Light of God's love in ways both time-tested and ever-new.

✤ Advent

The God who created us is the One who enters this world as Emmanuel offering the hope and forgiveness that makes us whole. The love of God is gracious and great, bold and boundless.

✤ Advent

With the birth of a Savior in Bethlehem, God entered our lives forever. There is no greater assurance of our Creator's steadfast love.

✤ Christmas

Whenever we are insecure in our faith, whenever we fall into spiritual neglect or disrepair, God reaches out to steady us and to embrace us with sure and complete forgiveness.

Though there are hindrances to a full understanding of God's presence in our lives, the light of divine love cannot be extinguished. It will reach us and illumine us, bearing witness to the Creator's mercy and grace and power.

The confidence that Christ's followers can have is grounded in the assurance of full forgiveness and steadfast love, and it is rightly focused on bringing to fruition all hopes that align with God's will.

The scriptures proclaim that God created us; the apostle Paul states that Christ is at work within us; the sharing of life in the church affirms that the Spirit is alive among us. All these things are very good news indeed.

The God whose children we are and whose creation we inhabit extends to us a forgiveness that is thorough and gracious. This forgiveness reveals the character of God's love; reflect upon it as you receive it throughout the Lenten season.

❖ Ash Wednesday
❖ Lent

The most profound and wondrous assurance of all time is that which is stated in the formative words of our faith: "Christ is risen!" Because Christ lives, *we* live as people loved and forgiven, people graced with the Spirit of service and peace.

❖ Easter

It does not get any simpler than this. We are called to follow where God leads, to love one another as God loves us. When we fall, we are picked up; when we fail, we are forgiven. Joyfully live the faith.

To all who seek and strive, God offers guidance and extends support. To all who journey with Jesus, God provides the companionship of the Holy Spirit. That is the way with our Creator's love.

Our God is gracious indeed. This very moment, may the steadfast love and thorough forgiveness of our Creator grant us a new start on the week ahead, on the rest of our lives.

Whether we are having a good cry in time of grief and trial or having a good laugh on an occasion of mirth and celebration, we know that God is with us. It is the steadfast, sustaining love of our Creator that we can trust as a reliable source of potent consolation, as a genuine cause for joy.

The poet Gerard Manley Hopkins wrote that the "world is charg'd with the grandeur of God." He might also have said that the world is made grand by the challenges of God...to live gracefully, to enjoy creation, to love one another. It is to these things that God calls us, and it is by the Spirit's power that we achieve the fulfillment of our faith.

It is a central joy of our faith that God is both reliable and loving. God will support us, guide us, and inspire us all of our days.

Whenever we fail or fall, we can rely upon the grace and forgiveness of God to help us gain balance and direction, to set us aright.

In confession, we approach God on the level of grace; through forgiveness, God reveals a capacity for love and healing that empowers us to action, that moves us to voice our grateful praise.

Our God reaches toward us in love, seeks to be found, and rejoices when grace given becomes a gift received. For the faith that touches and fulfills our lives, we offer thanks to God.

Our God abounds with love for all humankind and reveals that by empowering us with a spirit of compassion that can bring change for the better into this world.

Our God is One who lifts up those who are downcast, who unburdens those who are heavy laden, who enlightens those who dwell in darkness. It is by God's grace we know forgiveness, mercy, and joy.

It is God's joy to forgive. It is our joy to offer thanks in response.

The God who created us, who remains on listening and speaking terms with us through all circumstances, who opens the future to us, abounds with forgiving love. Receiving it, we can proclaim with joy: All thanks and glory be to God.

When we speak with God, we hear the needs of others more clearly. When we listen to God, we come to know ourselves. Such is the wondrous love of our Creator.

Nothing, the apostle Paul tells us, can separate us from the love of God in Christ Jesus. On this we can rely now and forever.

The apostle Paul assured the congregants of a church in Galatia that it is "For freedom Christ has set us free" (Galatians 5:1). Claiming that freedom, we acknowledge God's power of forgiveness and steadfast love.

"In the beginning was the Word, and the Word was with God, and the Word was God" (John 1:1). Now the Word speaks to us and through us; and whenever the noise of this world threatens to drown it out, we hear God's Word anew...in the encouragement of others; in calls that beckon us to service; in the still, small voice of forgiveness and grace.

To the hearing of our Creator, prayer is as the sound of music. God listens attentively, responds graciously, and invites encores and new compositions of prayerful expression.

Our God moves with power and grace in our lives, forgiving us and freeing us, loving us always.

Our Creator maintains a contact with us that is constant and loving, filled with the spirit of relentless forgiveness and dream-driven hope.

Where the love of God dwells, forgiveness has its home. Open yourselves to that love and live as people forgiven.

In times of turbulence, upset, or dismay, or at any time when we find ourselves foundering as individuals or as a people, it is the love of our faith's founder, Jesus of Nazareth, that will comfort and strengthen us without fail.

There is no greater good than the goodness of God, no forgiveness more thorough, no love more attentive, no power more enabling. All thanks be to God.

The surest sign of divine grace and greatness is the steadfast love that marks God's response to us in all circumstances. With constancy and compassion, our Creator draws us near that we may receive the gifts of forgiveness and new life.

God is at work as a power of healing within us and within the world; through the practice of our faith, we cooperate with our Creator and serve as conveyors of grace.

By the love of God we are created, by the mercy of God we are set free, by the grace of God we are given the time of our lives.

The God of all creation invites us to come near, to be in relation to our faith as a sojourner and not a tourist. God welcomes us to table, graces us with forgiveness, and establishes a continuing connection of love.

✤ Communion

God bids us to differ from those whose allegiances lie elsewhere. We are called to practice love with daring and with confidence; we are promised an empowering forgiveness and a sustaining grace.

The call to faithfulness is one that has reached out from the beginnings of creation. Each one of us continues to hear it as an invitation, a beckoning, an opportunity. It is indeed an ongoing gift of steadfast love.

It is the grace and power of God that draws us together, that inspires us to be gracious in our responsiveness to the needs of others, to be powerful in the practice of love as the foundation for faithful living. In a spirit of gratitude, we relax and rejoice in the presence of God.

When we confess our faults and sins, when we acknowledge our needs and name our hopes, God listens. And when we listen with all our minds, hearts, and spirits, we will hear the good news of God's love for us, and we can open ourselves to its guiding power.

The basic premises and promises of our faith are these: God loves us, forgives us, and sets us free. To spread that love, respond to that forgiveness, and share that freedom is the mission to which we are called. All thanks and glory be to God.

Where the love of God is, faith can come to fruition. And by the grace of God, that love is available everywhere, accessible to everyone.

Our God provides nourishment to sharpen spiritual senses. At the Lord's table of grace, we receive food for faith and community in Christ.

♣ Communion

Through participation in the life of the church, we identify ourselves as members of a faith family. In our work and play, struggles and successes, doubts and hopes, the Spirit dwells in our midst as a presence and a power.

In the midst of our struggles, when we feel unstable in spirit or unable to continue our journey of faith, God reaches toward us with the support of forgiving love.

The God who blesses us with treasures of sense and spirit is the One who urges and empowers us to grow in faith.

Our God has a divine devotion to hope. When it dares little, God challenges it; when it loses strength, God fortifies it. When it wanders, God redirects it; when it ceases, God revives it. Thanks be to God.

For the many gifts of God, we offer many thanks. And for the extensiveness of God's love, we offer to extend ourselves in service to others. It is right and just and joyous to do these things.

PRAYERS OF DEDICATION

Some of us are inclined to squander money. Some of us are committed to squirreling it away. Some of us see it as the means for enabling material acquisition. Some of us see it as a tool for empowering charitable inclinations. Some of us have little money. Some of us have a great deal.

During worship, the time of collection/offering makes it quite clear that how we regard money and what we do with it are not items to be treated with spiritual indifference. If, truly, all we have is ours by the grace of God, then it certainly matters what we do with it. All of it.

I consider the collection/offering as symbolic (as well as practical). It is our opportunity to take what the world values and to acknowledge its source. The prayer we say makes the point precisely: our giving is an act of *dedication*. Of self and substance. Of what we treasure and who we are.

Prayers of dedication serve to convey gratitude for the blessings granted by our Creator and to affirm that generosity, as we choose to enact it, is the best response to the graciousness and love of God. The tone of these prayers is fittingly one of reflective joy.

A point of information: The prayers of dedication offered in this section of the book are intended for general use throughout the church year. When a particular piece is specific to a holiday or occasion, it is noted.

Gracious God, implant within us the kind of generosity that surprises our spirits, enlivens our faith, strengthens our mission. Permit us through our giving to prepare the way for One whose realm and reign we honor. Amen.

✤ Advent

Loving God, we look toward the advent of our Messiah with hopeful anticipation. During this season of promise, inhabit our hearts as an indwelling power, and inspire us to prayerful gratitude and joyful generosity. Within our waiting and through our giving, let your Spirit act. May all our offerings be acceptable in your sight. In Jesus' name, Amen.

✤ Advent

O God, you did not have to come among us boldly. We do not have to give generously. But life is an adventure and a miracle. So you did come, out of love; and we do give, out of gratitude. Accept our offerings and our prayer, both presented in the name of Jesus Christ. Amen.

✤ Advent

Creator God, you sent your Child to be with us as One who proclaimed and enacted the good Word of your love for all humankind. From him we learned the world-shaping, life-changing power of that love. This time of Advent, inhabit our hearts and direct our life together. Help us to put your Word into action, to speak it through service and to give it volume through our giving. In the name of Jesus Christ, Amen.

✤ Advent

Loving God, may the offerings we make today carry to others glad tidings of peace, tidings of comfort and joy. Let our generosity be as great as it would if we were kneeling before the Christchild on the night of his birth. Receive our gifts as carols of praise and statements of faith. In Jesus' name we pray. Amen.

✤ Advent

Gracious God, as we receive with gratitude your Christmas presence, grant us the wisdom to understand that you have made this world your realm. Through the gifts we offer, the love we expend, the faith we practice, enable us to participate in the glorious work of doing your will on Earth. In the name of Jesus Christ, Amen.

✤ Christmas

Gracious God, for what you have accomplished in our lives over the past year, we give our thanks. And for your promise to accompany us through the discoveries of the coming year, we also give our thanks. Receive our gratitude as expressed through these offerings, and hear our prayerful petition that you challenge us with change and sustain us with your support in time ahead. In Jesus' name, Amen.

✤ New Year

Loving God, we know no worthier cause than meeting needs in the name and for the sake of Christ. Use these gifts to extend our faith's caring through the work of a charitable, compassionate and creative church. We pray in Jesus' name. Amen.

O God, in the realm of fiscal affairs, we concern ourselves with stocks and bonds and various securities. In the spiritual realm, you bid us take stock of our motives and actions, hold fast to the bonds of community, and find in your grace the security we seek. As we offer our gifts, we pray that our spirits attach to you. In Jesus' name, Amen.

Loving God, as we develop attitudes that guide us in our giving, help us to be scripturally astute, spiritually attentive, and socially aware. Enable us through these offerings to respond to your Word with a measure of true faithfulness. In Jesus' name, Amen.

O God, we offer these gifts gladly for it is our pleasure to serve. Move us to a generosity that expresses the joy within that allows the laughter of our spirits to enhance the well-being of your church. Accept these offerings, we pray, as we present them in the name of Jesus Christ. Amen.

O God, as followers of Christ and as members of the human family, we bring forward these gifts in your honor and in service to our brothers and sisters. And we ask that you encourage us to offer not only these things of value, but also to contribute our values themselves to meet the world's needs. May all our gifts and our giving be acceptable in your sight. In the name of Jesus Christ. Amen.

Gracious God, when we look upon all the things that our offerings support, help us to see beyond programs and wages, maintenance and supplies. Enable us to see Jesus, alive in the work and worship of this church, present in our gathering and our giving. In his name we pray. Amen.

Gracious God, as we present these offerings, enable us to regard the church as though it were a child entrusted to our care. Help us to envision its brightest future, enact its highest hopes, preserve its ongoing health, support its steadfast growth. May our gifts serve to nurture the church as it bears witness to your Child in whose name we pray. Amen.

O God, in presenting these offerings as symbols of praise and signs of faith, we pray that they mark our commitment to spend ourselves as well as our substance for you. You spared no expense in purchasing for us forgiveness, hope, and new life. May our generosity be as yours. In the name of Jesus Christ. Amen.

We see you, O God, everywhere we turn, and we know that it is because of you that our lives are made full. As the church gathers together in your name, we offer you these gifts and our lives. Work through these gifts that lives may be touched by your grace and love, for it is in giving to others that we give our thanks to you. In Jesus' name. Amen.

God our Creator and Provider, there is no s
ing for the extent of your forgiveness and mercy anc
only acknowledge the abundance, receive with 1.
respond with faithful service. These things we do gladl
fully in the name of Jesus Christ. Amen.

Gracious God, knowing that you never withdraw your love
from us, we entrust our lives into your safekeeping, offer our
resources for your use, and invest our effort toward the upbuilding
of your reign and realm. Inspire us to generosity and fullness of
faith. In our Savior's name we pray. Amen.

O God, as we recognize the richness of our blessings, you
afford us the opportunity to develop the generosity that marks true
faithfulness. May our distribution of material wealth signify the
extent of our spiritual discernment and health. In the name of Jesus
Christ. Amen.

Gracious God, we realize that when we are attentive to your
will, we are less retentive of our resources. And we know that when
our giving is truly inspired, you provide us with a wealth of spiritual
satisfactions. In good faith, we present these offerings and ask that
you guide their use. In Jesus' name we offer our prayer. Amen.

Gracious God, we derive from the fare of our Lord's table
nourishment for our spirits. And we sense in our sharing the fond
fellowship of faith. With gratitude for these things we have received,
we offer our gifts, our praise, our commitment to serve well in
Christ's name. Amen.

♣ Communion

Gracious God, let these gifts we offer be as living water for
the church. Use them as support for this congregation's programs
and projects, as a source of energy for our outreach and wider ministry, as refreshment for our spirits in their growth toward greater
generosity and compassion. May all our gifts flow forth from the
deep well of faith. In the name of Jesus Christ. Amen.

O God, through these offerings, bring a more complete awareness of the wonder that is your love for us; and through them, too,
allow the love we have for others to come to expression. Fill us with
a Christlike generosity of spirit. In the name of our Savior we pray.
Amen.

O God, because life is your gift to us, we give with gratitude.
Because freedom is your gift to us, we give with gladness. May we
be graceful and generous in our giving as you are in yours. In the
name of Jesus Christ we pray. Amen.

Loving God, you have provided us with the talents and skills
that create our earning-power. We pray that you nurture within us
the grace and spirit that develop our giving-power. Grant us the
wisdom to define our riches by the offerings we make in Christ's
name. Amen.

God of grace and glory, we ask that you use our offerings to
strengthen this church, to amplify its voicing of good news, to
encourage its daring of faith through deeds of love. Accept our gifts
as expressions of commitment to the ways of Jesus Christ. In his
name we pray. Amen.

Generous God, it is quite a spread that you set before us this
morning: the bread of life and the cup of blessing. These things, lovingly prepared and graciously given by Jesus himself, nourish our
spirits and equip us for service in the world. Help us now to spread
before others these offerings we make, to distribute them with a
Christly kind of love and care. We pray in the name of the One at
whose table we gather. Amen.

✣ Communion

Loving God, these gifts represent a portion of our material
earnings and they signify the presence within us of spiritual yearnings. May our heartfelt gratitude and our growing faith merge in the
act of generous giving. We ask this in the name of Jesus Christ.
Amen.

Loving God, this presentation of gifts is but a moment in the service of worship, but our offering of self and substance goes far beyond the momentary. We are entirely yours, O God, so send us to meet any needs you discern and spend us as you will. May all our gifts and our giving be acceptable in your sight. In Jesus' name. Amen.

O God, you come near to us as the taste of bread in our mouths, the coursing of blood through our bodies, the moving of holy imagination that dwells within our spirits. May your loving closeness enable us to be generous and helpful of heart and hand. Accept our gifts, we pray, offered in the name of Jesus Christ. Amen.

✣ Communion

Good and gracious God, source of all our resources, teach us to serve you with generosity generation upon generation. Turn our intentions into offerings and our hopes into actions. Enable us to grow in faithfulness through the practice of giving. In Jesus' name we pray. Amen.

Teach us, O God, to linger with our giving. Help us to avoid any haste that prevents a maturing of generosity. Grant us the patience to allow our love to ripen into deed. And use these offerings over time as proclamations of your sovereignty in our lives. In Jesus' name, Amen.

Loving God, you have provided us with prayer as a place of spiritual retreat and sanctuary. Yet it is in prayer that our understandings advance and our service gains boldness. You have provided us with giving as a way of offering quiet thanks for blessings received; let giving also be for us a loud proclamation of our values and hopes. In the name of Jesus Christ. Amen.

Loving God, we acknowledge that you have far less interest in our incomes than in our expenditures, far less interest in the valuables we receive than the values we express. You are the source of all we have. May we be the source of what you need to extend your love throughout the Earth. Accept our offerings, we pray, as we give them in the name of Jesus Christ. Amen.

Loving God, let these offerings serve as connecting links between the effort that goes into our everyday occupations and the labor that upbuilds your eternal realm, between the hopes that energize our spirits and the satisfactions that develop when beliefs become deeds. Use these gifts to your glory. In the name of Jesus Christ we pray. Amen.

Loving God, inspire us to offer more than fragments of faithfulness, more than tiny portions of our talents, more than the monetary and spiritual equivalent of spare change. Help us to dare change for your sake, to live by grace and to enjoy the benefits of generosity. We ask this in the name of him who is our model of self-giving, Jesus the Christ. Amen.

Loving God, you provide us with life and you restore our souls, you extend forgiveness and you enable growth, you call us by name and you invite us to supper at your table. Accept our offerings, we pray, as our grateful response to grace granted and to gifts received. In the name of Jesus Christ, Amen.

✣ Communion

Loving God, turn these gifts to your purposes. Use them to enable deeds of sanctity in a world profaned by injustice and unconcern; use them to create a context of sanctuary for persons sorrowful or distressed. We ask this in the name of Jesus Christ, whose holiness and compassion our faith strives to enact. Amen.

Loving God, whenever we make offerings in Christ's name and for the church's use, let it be with the sense of joy derived from generosity. Remove any hindrances or restraints that prevent us from knowing the spiritual gladness of abundant giving. With thanks for all we have received, we extend our prayer and praise. Amen.

O God, help our love come to expression through these offerings. As they give voice to your Word in the world, let them become as couplets of compassion and sonnets of service. We pray in the name of him whose love shapes our life together, Jesus our Redeemer. Amen.

O God, may these coins be signs of our commitment, these dollars symbols of our devotion, these checks reminders of our choice to serve you above all. Lead us, we pray, in the ways of love and charity, for we acknowledge that our giftedness has its source in your grace. May our offerings of self and substance be acceptable in your sight. In Jesus' name, Amen.

O God, as we offer this money to further the work of your church, we ask that you grant us ever-new ways of offering ourselves as well as our substance.

Open us to full appreciation of our giftedness, and unwrap our time, talents and commitment, so that in your receiving them our joy of giving might be complete. We ask this in the name of Jesus Christ. Amen.

God of tender power and bold compassion, your love defines as our neighbors all persons in need. Your grace opens Christ's table to all who hunger for mercy and who thirst for peace. Grant us the generosity to create a global neighborhood. And grant us the wisdom to learn at table a lesson of acceptance and sharing. Use as you will our gifts and our giving. In Jesus' name, Amen.

♣ Communion

O God, through the offering of these gifts may we become a more open people. Help us to be open-minded in hearing your Word and wisdom, open-hearted in healing a broken world, open-handed in heeding your call for charity and enacted love. With thanks for all good gifts, we present a portion of our substance and the whole of ourselves. In Jesus' name, Amen.

Loving God, we pray that you accept every contribution we make as the renewal of our commitment to serve you. And we ask that you use all our offerings to give voice to your values through the work of this church. In the earnest hope that your will may be done on Earth, we pray in Jesus' name. Amen.

O God, grant that we who have received so much come to experience generous giving as a saving grace. Permit us, through offerings of what we treasure, to follow Christ's example of sacrificial love and to express our faith with heartfelt devotion. Increase our joy as we present our gifts to you. In Jesus' name we pray. Amen.

Gracious God, with these gifts come our hopes that the church grow in wisdom and fellowship, that it find direction in the practice of prayer and fulfillment, in bold acts of mercy and justice. Use our gifts to help bring to fruition the hopes of others throughout your world. Accept this offering, we pray, as a commitment of dedicated service. In the name of Jesus Christ, Amen.

O God, we offer for the ministry of this church a portion of our earnings; we offer as a response to your grace the whole of ourselves. Your love is an incoming power upon which we rely. May our gifts be a reliable source of empowerment for the church. In the name of Jesus Christ we pray. Amen.

O God, each item put into these offering plates is an expression of our gratitude to you. Increase both our sensitivity to your grace and our readiness to say thank you. May all our gifts and our giving be acceptable in your sight. In the name of Jesus Christ, Amen.

PASTORAL PRAYERS

*T*he pastoral prayer is essentially a "caretaker's prayer." Clergy offer it as a means of expressing care about parishioners' needs, care about a world filled with traumas and pains and crises, care about those things that separate us in any way from God. The pastoral prayer is, at its best, care-full (carrying our abundant needs to God), but never careful (in the sense of backing away from what might be considered incidental or far distant, overwhelming or off-putting). Pastoral prayers serve as expressions of spiritual boldness by affirming a thorough trust in God's responsive, guiding and steadfast love. In this, they may be considered descendants of the writings of the psalmists and prophets.

The examples I offer in the section of the book that follows provide templates for construction of pastoral prayers. Some of them are suitable for use intact while others serve better when modified to suit local occasions, situations, and needs.

O God, we offer our prayer in unity of spirit.

Grant us in days to come a full understanding of what it means to belong to you; help us to see that being your child sets us free to love, to practice compassion, to work for justice.

Build in us humble spirits that enable us to look upon all persons as equals. Generate in us the energy and courage that will make us peacemakers and healers in ways that you will call blessed.

In the season of Advent ahead, as we reflect upon and pray for the church, increase our appreciation for the diversity that makes it whole, the variety of traditions that provide it wisdom, the power of the Spirit that gives it unity.

Draw us together, we pray, to serve better and to worship with greater devotion. And now, joining our voices with others, we speak the words of Jesus Christ who was One for all persons in all times, who taught us his prayer saying... [the prayer of Jesus]. Amen.

✤ Advent
✤ Peace
✤ Unity

God of Advent hope, help us this season to receive Christ anew. Though the carols will be familiar, the story will be one we have heard countless times before, and the celebrations will be shaped by tradition, open us to understandings surprising and fresh.

We often forget that your arrival as an infant was more improbable than predictable. And we tend to confine our feelings about the coming of Christ to small interior places. Grant us, we pray, spirits awakened, startled and struck by the wonder of your love. Fill us with the kind of joy that resounds with your praise, that stretches horizon to horizon across our lives.

Lead us to accept the presence of Christ as a call to enflesh our beliefs, to let a body of deeds form around the framework of faithfulness. Our world needs all the love and compassion we can muster, for conflicts rage among and within nations, physical ailments and diseased systems plague multitudes of people, abuses of defenseless individuals and fragile environments abound, dishonesties and injustices seem to flourish, prejudices lurk. Fill us with the spiritual courage to address issues with prayer and with action. Instead of offering commentary on the problems we see, enable us to offer energetic commitment. Move us this Advent closer to Christ, closer to a faith incarnate and alive with the power to accomplish change by your grace and to your glory.

We pray in the name of Jesus Christ. Amen.

✤ Advent
✤ Justice
✤ Hope

Gracious God, last week we lit the light of hope. We anticipate the coming of Christ with hope in our hearts...hope for healing of those who hurt due to the destruction wrought by disease or war or internal struggles, hope for growth in our awareness of your will and in our commitment to justice, hope for rebirth and renewal of commitment to those we love, hope for strengthened spirits, hope for joy's extension into days ahead. Remind us, we pray, in times when the world seems bent on dashing hope, that you keep calling us to go on daring hope. Brighten our lives with the assurance of your promise and your presence.

Empowering God, this week we lit the light of peace. We anticipate the coming of Christ with peace in our hearts...peace that moves us to become skillful reconcilers and seekers of common ground, peace that takes form in the practice of prayer and the dismantling of conflict's causes, peace that beckons us to work at eliminating abuses of power and at transforming unjust systems and at changing minds and hearts, peace that roots itself deeply in your holy love. Remind us, we pray, in times when the world seems filled with warring madness, in hills far away and on the streets of this land, that you bid us walk in the ways of a servant Savior. Brighten our lives with the comfort of your promise and your presence.

Help us throughout the remainder of the Advent season to carry within us the love of Christ, to let our lives bear joyful witness to your grace and power. Amen.

✤ Advent
✤ Peace
✤ Faith, practice of

O God, as Christmas draws nearer, allow our spirits to open up, to expand with wonder, to stretch out in love, to grow in wisdom. Let this season be one of grace and joy.

We offer our thanks for your coming among us. How complete your love that you risked putting on humanity. We confess that sometimes in our selfishness or fear we desire to put you off, to pretend that you do not know our feelings, our hopes, our fears. Be patient with us, we pray; forgive our drawing back and gently remind us that Emmanuel was born to be with us always.

Enable us during the final days of Advent and in time beyond the celebration of Jesus' birth to be active in our longing to know you. Charge us to be receptive to your presence in our lives, to have as our models the exultant shepherds, the obedient parents, the journeying Magi. Help us to realize that you reveal yourself constantly; help us to rejoice in that.

Hear our prayer of concern and caring for those whose lives are tormented by hunger, anguished by grief, bound by oppression, pained by illness, or strained by hard decisions and struggles within. Grant them your comfort, your healing, your assurance of steadfast love and presence. Now, as we name these people silently, hear our prayer...

We pray in the name of Jesus Christ and share his words together saying... [the prayer of Jesus]. Amen.

✤ Advent
✤ Incarnation
✤ God, love of

O God, we join together in prayer on this holy eve asking that the Spirit of Christmas dwell in us and act upon us according to our need.

Where there is pain or despondency, may the Spirit come with brightness and may the touch of the Child be one of healing.

Where there is aimlessness, may the Spirit be as a star giving direction and drawing us onward.

Where belief is scant and faith is weak, may the Spirit take us to the manger where we have our surprising beginnings as believers and as people of faith.

Where selfishness exists, may the Spirit grant us wisdom like that of the magi, enabling us to give with generosity and with an attitude of worship.

Where values are confused, may the Spirit of Christmas set them aright, for in this season we are shown that which is most valuable... the opportunity to offer you glory and praise, the chance to affirm a sense of family that is holy, the knowledge that the Bearer of peace is truly among us.

We pray in the name of the Christmas Child who grew to be our Sovereign and Savior. Amen.

❖ Christmas Eve
❖ Christmas, Spirit of
❖ Healing

Loving God, you came among us in the person of Jesus to know this world's joys and tribulations, to feel its hungers and hurts, to foster growth in spirit and in truth. Today we offer our prayer for the people of this world whose lives reflect a human neglect and call out for the touch of your compassion and justice.

Turn our active attention and your great love toward those for whom we pray...

✝ toward all casualties of war and victims of environmental devastation

✝ toward any persons society regards as unsightly and so condemns to the status of out-of-sight-out-of-mind

✝ toward those at ease with their plenty in a world of want

✝ toward all sufferers of physical disease, emotional distress, spiritual listlessness

✝ toward persons struggling to make whole a life fragmented by any form of abuse

✝ toward those distanced by prejudice or written off as "not our kind"

✝ toward all imprisoned by physical walls, by imposed systems of injustice, by their own lack of confidence or hope

✝ toward friends or family members whose problems weigh upon them.

We pray boldly, for we trust in your power, mercy and grace. And we pray in the name of our Savior. Amen.

❖ Incarnation
❖ Justice
❖ Healing

Loving God, we come to you with our concerns for the world and with a world of joys.

We ask for the devotion and discipline to participate daily, through prayer, in the process of building peace. Let us begin with the simple recognition that all persons are truly sisters and brothers in the one human family that is your creation. Help us to know in our hearts that neither distances nor differences can be allowed to keep us from feeling the hurts of others. Whether the violence be domestic or the strife international, whether the wounds be fresh and physical or the scars deep and internal, we seek the power of your presence and the balm of your love. Grant us, too, we pray, the courage to be healers in this world, agents of your grace in every situation of our lives, in every contact we have.

Creator God, we give you praise and thanks for the wonders of this world, those things that bless and enrich our lives...plants that give us breath and animals that give us companionship, water that refreshes us and oranges that taste of stored sunshine, memories and miracles in family life, friendship bursting with meaning and beauty, time cherished for what it held, powerful prayers steeped in quietness, glimpses of your Spirit in action. So much is given us. Increase and enlarge our appreciation as we offer thanks to you.

Concerns we bring before you with confidence; joys we name with a sense of gratitude. Hear us as we pray in silence....

[silent prayer]

In the name of Jesus Christ we pray. Amen.

✤ Peace
✤ Joy
✤ World, concern for

Loving God, we pray this morning for peace.

Let it begin within each one of us as we commit ourselves to praying for enemies, seeking reconciliation with those against whom we hold grudges or resentments or hatreds. May the breaking of bread at table signify our willingness to break away from any bondage to revenge.

Allow your peace to thrive in families as they work through the conflicts and disagreements of daily life shared together. Make healing ever-accessible and let forgiveness become a practiced instrument of grace. Use your peace to dissolve the antagonisms and misunderstandings that sometimes mark the relationships between people who differ in political view, economic status, religious belief, racial make-up or sexual orientation. May the breaking of bread draw us together and alert us to our common humanity, and may the first impulse of our spirits be toward serving one another.

Bring your peace to bear wherever there is active strife or the threat of war…[name areas around the world where turmoil is present]. May harmony replace animosity as a reigning power in every region of your Earth. Let the broken bread nourish us to work for peace in the world. We pray in Jesus Christ's good name. Amen.

✤ Peace
✤ Communion
✤ Forgiveness

Loving God, we offer thanks this day for the church – body of Christ, vessel of the Spirit, family of faith, witness in the world.

Help us to consider Christ in all we do, letting our decisions be made as with his mind, our relationships be formed as with his heart, our deeds be done as with his hands.

Encourage us to go where the Spirit moves us, individually and as a congregation, opening ourselves to the possibilities of service that you imagine for us and equip us to accomplish.

Strengthen us as a family of faith, bonding us in mutual support, guiding us toward steadfast love of our children and youth, keeping us close to you.

And enable us to be bold witnesses, for we know that the world is in need of good news and we sense in our spirits the importance of conveying your love to all persons.

Hear our prayer, words offered in gratitude and praise, confidence and trust, all in the name of Jesus Christ. Amen.

✤ Church
✤ Mission
✤ Faith, family of

O God, make us your bearers and shapers of hope. Attune us to the needs of sisters and brothers who clamor for justice, mercy, and peace. Broaden our compassion for neighbors near and far whose burdens, pains, and afflictions we are called to share. Strengthen the connections that bind together all who follow Christ.

You teach us, loving God, that if we would be people of hope, we must be people of courage who observe with keenness of spirit, pray with intensity, act with humble righteousness. Charge us with an understanding of resurrection power as present and accessible, and prompt us to derive from that understanding the energy to do your will.

Enable us to serve you well by working with others to obtain what they need most deeply...

For the hurt – healing	For the healthy – gratitude
For the grieving – support	For the joyful – mission
For the oppressed – release	For the satisfied – humility
For the downcast – empathy	For the upbeat – direction
For the rejected – good news	For the comfortable – commitment

Hear our prayer, O God, offered with hope in the name of Jesus Christ, who bid us pray together saying... [the prayer of Jesus]. Amen.

✤ Hope
✤ Mission
✤ Justice

Gracious God, help us to see. Heal the blindnesses that go by many names...apathy and prejudice, practiced selfishness and simple inattention. Grant us the wisdom and humility to allow Jesus to touch our lives in a way that clears our vision and cleanses our spirits.

Help us to see the pains that afflict persons near and dear to us; teach us to be able in the ministry of compassion.

Help us to see the paths of service you set before us; urge us to identify our gifts toward the end of using them in ways that are pleasing in your sight.

Help us to see goodness and to refrain from judgment; enable us to build partnerships and cooperative relationships with people who exercise a Christly power of healing.

Help us to see through prayer the world hidden from our sight, the world of brothers and sisters deeply in need of our love and our abundance; encourage us to expand one great hour into an ongoing commitment of sharing.

Help us to see the mysteries visible only to the eyes of faith; fill us with grace, temper us with mercy, toughen us with justice, imbue us with peace, and enfold us in the love that will not let us go.

We offer our prayer in the name of Jesus Christ, whose words we now say together.... [the prayer of Jesus]. Amen.

❖ One Great Hour of Sharing
❖ Mission
❖ Faith, vision of

Loving God, throughout this Lenten season take hold of our faith. Shape it, be its source of strength.

May our faith put on a quality of serenity that enables us to cherish the silent workings of prayer and to pursue justice with unruffled courage.

May our faith develop a sensibility that feels deeply the brokenness of others and that touches the hurts of this world with tenderness and healing.

May our faith adopt a commitment to service that energizes our fellowship and that leads us into the kind of mission efforts that build peace and facilitate reconciliation.

May our faith accept searching as a life task for all who wish to mature in spirit and to walk humbly with you.

We offer prayer this week especially for...[name needs].

In our prayer and contemplation, we hold these persons and situations in the light of your love.

All prayer we offer in the name of Jesus Christ, whose words we speak together saying... [the prayer of Jesus]. Amen.

❖ Lent
❖ Faith, components of
❖ Faith, growth of

O God, our Creator and Sustainer, you have been with us through all our history as individual persons and as people of the church. You remembered us especially when Jesus walked the Earth and put our lives in focus, and you remember us yet when your Spirit develops in ours the hopeful image of Christian life. Enlighten our outlook on the everyday by sharpening our awareness of your presence within it. When our activities are frantic or blurred, let our worship be a time of composure; when our lives seem undirected or our energies are dulled, let our worship be a time for getting on track and for renewing our store of excitement and joy. Help us daily to put aside those things that distract our attention from your ways and will – fill us with a sense of worship through all our days.

As you are with us and within us, give us the strength to live for you. And make us one as followers of Jesus Christ. Amen.

✤ Lent
✤ Faith, power of
✤ Worship

Loving God, we pray this morning with a forthright simplicity.

Help us to seek after your wisdom with urgency of hope and gentleness of pace.

Teach us to extend healing whenever we see tears of pain or signs of long-endured sufferings.

Enable us to respond to needs by envisioning possibilities beyond the limitations of human systems and structures.

Urge us to catch the joy of faith's fellowship and of your Spirit's presence within our solitude.

Inspire us to solve insurmountable problems by an acceptance of grace and a reliance on your power.

Fill us with a reverence for life and a deep appreciation for our gifts, our faith, our future.

We pray in the name of Jesus Christ whose words we share saying... [the prayer of Jesus]. Amen.

✤ Lent
✤ Simplicity
✤ Faith, power of

O God, we give thanks for the courage of Jesus Christ as he risked himself not just for the sake of getting a message across, but for the sake of touching each and every one of us with your love. Grant us the courage to follow our Savior's example, to move beyond the celebration of this day to the daily demonstration of holy living.

As we welcome the presence of Christ within us, we discover a new base of operations and a new way of seeing and doing. Although we often find it awkward to make an acceptance of your will the starting point for action, we seek to become graceful. Through the practice of our faith, help us to experience for ourselves and to extend to others your thorough forgiveness, gentle power, healing compassion, steadfast love.

We know, O God, persons hurting in body, struggling with decisions, searching for answers. We know situations around the world where the pain that people feel demands the heartfelt application by followers of Christ of your caring, justice and peace. The needs cry out as loudly as did the Jerusalem crowd long ago, yet we hold them before you now in the sincerity and serenity of silent prayer... [name needs].

We pray in the name of Jesus Christ, who guided us toward holy living when he bid us pray together saying.... [the prayer of Jesus]. Amen.

✤ Palm Sunday
✤ Faith, practice of
✤ Mission

O God of Easter promise and hope, enter our lives with resurrection power; grant to all persons an enthusiasm for life and a readiness to practice the love of Christ.

On this Easter day, we pray that many of the things we are prone to disbelieve be raised up as live possibilities.... By the power of the risen Christ, may we be enabled:

✝ to exist in harmony and balance with the natural world
✝ to share the good Earth in peace as brothers and sisters
✝ to work on the building up of your Realm
✝ to care passionately for the least and lowly
✝ to worship you with fitting joy and due honor.

Our praise this morning bursts forth like laughter and our gratitude on this day of resurrection grows within us as we share the prayer of our risen Savior... [the prayer of Jesus]. Amen.

✤ Easter
✤ Faith, possibilities of
✤ God, power of

Leading, guiding, course-setting God, we strive to entrust ourselves to you. And we acknowledge that this does not come easily. We have our own important agendas that too often exclude you, our own areas of concern that sometimes neglect or reject your call to place a priority on compassion, our own ways that regard your way as an unwelcome detour. Whenever we sense or feel these things, remind us that we are your own.

Grant us the courage and the wisdom…

+ to follow the Spirit into disciplines of personal prayer that challenge us to grow in faith and dislodge us from attachments to anything that stifles our souls

+ to follow the Spirit into paths of service that widen our sense of neighborhood and broaden our shoulders to bear burdens for those whose hunger, pain or weakness disables them

+ to follow the Spirit into dark places as bearers of light, as laborers working to shape brighter prospects of justice and peace and humane treatment for all persons

+ to follow the Spirit into regions of joy that defy understanding, laughter that has the quality of spontaneous childlike mirth, wonder that inspires us to explore and imagine and hope and create.

May your grace and love bud to new life, and may your Spirit surge within us. This we pray in the name of Jesus Christ. Amen.

❖ Pentecost
❖ Spirit, activity of
❖ Faith, disciplines of

O God, we have so many options of what we can choose to rule our lives and guide our actions. By your grace, you grant us the freedom of choice; by the wisdom of faith, may we follow the Christ's direction and the Spirit's way.

May we discover in times of solitude the quiet outreach you offer and the substantial support you lovingly provide.

May we express in our contacts with family and friends an openness to sharing ourselves and to receiving the gifts they have to share with us.

May we exercise our understanding of your love through the life and activity of this church.

May we envision a world in which justice and compassion and enduringly true peace are the order of the day, a world that proclaims with its very being the sovereignty of holy love. May we strive to put form to that vision as we couple our efforts with the Spirit's power to build a hopeful future.

We offer our prayer in the name of Jesus Christic. Amen.

✤ Hope
✤ Faith, practice of
✤ Faith, centrality of

O God, we pray this morning...

✚ for brothers and sisters in struggle with situations out of control or in the control of powers that foster chaos, we pray this morning...

✚ for brothers and sisters mired in situations that victimize whole groups or races, situations in which brutality is commonplace and random, we pray this morning...

✚ for brothers and sisters who struggle against despair or dark forces within themselves, against memories that linger but might better be let go, against destructive inclinations, we pray this morning...

✚ for brothers and sisters involved in the battle with disease, with difficult decisions that affect family and future, with pains of loss that divert attention from life's fullness, we pray this morning...

✚ for brothers and sisters who struggle to enact their fondest hopes for a more humane and just world, to use abilities to the utmost, to build the church into a community of caring and compassion.

For all these persons, our sisters and brothers, we ask the strengthening of your Spirit, in the name of Jesus Christ, ally of those who struggle and Savior in whose name we pray. Amen.

✤ Justice
✤ Faith, practice of
✤ Mission

Gracious God, we give our thanks this morning for the entire world, formed by your creative Spirit without boundary lines between nations, without prejudices between peoples, without divisions between what is ours and what is yours. Grant us, as we look upon the inhabitants and the events of this Earth, a sense of all-embracing love. Fill us with a courage to face the problems we see, a caring that moves us to action, a cooperativeness that opens up the prospect of genuine peace.

Shape your church into a model of unity and spiritual energy. Let this be a place where connections get made, connections internal and interpersonal. Help us to identify our needs and to hold them before you, to form our relationships around a commitment to serve you, to profess primary allegiance to you through every word and deed.

Inspire us and enable us to be whole as individuals and as a community. Urge us to integrate our abilities with our dreams, so that hopes not only draw forth our devotion but truly take form in our lives.

We pray in the name of Jesus Christ. Amen.

✤ Gratitude
✤ Faith, practice of
✤ God, reaching toward

O God, we offer this morning our thanks for a living church...

✤ a running, shouting, squirming church filled with children who learn from teachers and who teach all who seek to learn your ways;

✤ a worshiping church willing and able to voice praise, express concerns, hear needs;

✤ a changing church open to the Spirit's movement, the presence of new faces, the gifts of both tradition and innovation;

✤ a praying church responsive to your Word in ways that involve hearts and hands, minds and spirits;

✤ a doing church aware of the call to practice faith through action, to bear witness to your love and justice and compassion through spoken truth and caring deeds.

We pray with full gratitude in the name of Jesus Christ. Amen.

✤ Church
✤ Faith, activity/activities of
✤ Faith, character/characteristics of

O God, we thank you this morning for families...

For the guidance, support and discipline we receive through them, for the patience, acceptance and love they call upon us to give.

We give thanks for the variety of families...

For those small or extensive, for those blended or adoptive, for those headed by single parents or partners.

We pray for families in crisis:

May we minister to them with compassion and may your Spirit become a source of strength.

We pray for families apart:

Fill their members with a love that can reach over great distances and can transcend the hurts of a broken family-structure.

We pray for families growing in number or about to be formed through marriage:

Bless those newly added with a home, bless those who marry with a commitment to make intention reality.

We pray for families that are happy and prosperous of spirit:

Grant them continuing success and remind them that the joy they find in family life is a wealth to be shared.

We pray for durable families:

Hold them up as models of hope and of sustaining love.

And we pray for the faith family, giving thanks for the heritage it has provided, thanks for the promise it bears. Nurture us within it as we strive to be in all ways your faithful children, brothers and sisters of him who taught us his prayer, saying... [the prayer of Jesus]. Amen.

✤ Church
✤ Families
✤ Faith, family of

Loving God, we offer our prayer of thanks for this church, for its ministry to those with individual needs, for its outreach to our community through the addressing of challenging issues, for its conscience in responding to crises around the world. Grant us a breadth of vision and a depth of feeling that enable us to continue the exercise of compassion that is truly Christlike...intimate in its approach, noble in its intent, all-embracing in its scope.

Help us to be steadfast in the task of discipling our children, teaching them to value the dignity of others, to practice the love you place within them, to maintain an exuberance for service within the church.

Help us to use our talents to your glory and to the benefit of our neighbors, to follow the course of spiritual curiosity, to tend to the needs we see in your world, for it is – by your grace – our world as well.

Keep us active in worship and open to caring companionship with one another. Enable us to be keepers of faith in a culture that often demeans it, distorts it, rejects its power.

Remind us always to support one another, to be energetic in prayer. Relying upon you to hear us and to respond according to your will, we offer our prayer in Jesus' name. Amen.

✤ Church
✤ Faith, power of
✤ Faith, community of

Loving God, we give thanks this morning for the span of life, the wonder of creation, the bonds of friendship, the challenge of faith, the steadfastness of your presence.

Help us, we pray, to be responsible citizens of the Earth, to live lightly upon it, to consider it and value it as a living work of art, to plan its preservation, and to enjoy its gifts of beauty and recreation. Teach us to be perceptive observers of the natural world and to move from keen vision to wise insight as we come to see your glory revealed roundabout us.

For the whole of your human family we offer our words of concern and hope. Touch with your gracious and compassionate kindness those who are victimized by the greed or neglect of others, those who live where conflict or natural disasters threaten life, those who face decisions difficult and deep, those who reach to regain health, those who have the power yet lack the will to extend great service. We pray together as a caring community for persons close to us whose needs you know and whose names we voice now in silence...

O God, hear our prayer offered in the name of Jesus Christ, who taught us to come before you saying... [the prayer of Jesus]. Amen.

✤ Environment
✤ Faith, family of
✤ Mission

Loving God, we have much to be thankful for this day...

✛ for a congregation alive and thriving;
✛ for the company and support of good friends in the community of faith;
✛ for children who help us clarify our beliefs and values;
✛ for the gifts of scripture and Spirit that prompt and enable our actions;
✛ for a capacity to enjoy life and to savor service done in Christ's name;
✛ for the willingness to face injustices with repentance and courage;
✛ for the coming of a Savior who will be for us a wonderful counselor and maker of peace.

It is with abundant gratitude in our hearts that we continue our prayer in silence...
[silence]

We pray in the name of Jesus Christ, whose words we share saying... [the prayer of Jesus]. Amen.

✤ Thanksgiving
✤ Faith, basics of
✤ Mission

Loving God, we give thanks this day that you are the God of revelation, for your will to be known by us.

Creative and renewing God, we rejoice in the variety of ways you call us into relationship with you.

For a natural world that beckons us to appreciation and to gentleness, we offer thanks...

For faces that show the need for love, the yearnings for peace, the power of hope, the strength of faith, we offer thanks...

For bold prophets and courageous reconcilers, we offer thanks...

For everyday work and unusual opportunities, we offer thanks...

For strains of music that uplift us and harmonies of spirit that comfort us, we offer thanks...

For churches that serve as home bases of inspiration and community, we offer thanks...

For all these, we offer thanks.

Through them your image comes to clarity and we become more able servants of the One who bore your image among us and who taught us to pray together saying... [the prayer of Jesus]. Amen.

✣ Thanksgiving
✣ Faith, practice of
✣ Church

SPECIAL OCCASION PRAYERS

$\mathcal{A}$lthough every opportunity to engage in worship and to offer prayer may be considered a special occasion, certain events call for prayers marked by highly specific focus. These are prayers of many varieties...thanksgiving, petition, blessing, intercession.

In the section of the book that follows, I offer samples of prayers composed for particular events. They follow in the tradition of "occasional poems," written to commemorate notable activities or achievements: coronations, memorials, baptisms, weddings, military ceremonies, graduations, awards. The prayers and liturgical pieces I have written by no means cover the full range of special occasions meriting spiritual attention. But though their scope is not exhaustive, they do provide examples of how we address and reach toward God with targeted intent.

※

Advent Candle-Lighting
(text and prayers to be used especially with children present)

First Sunday

Today is the first day of the season called Advent. The word Advent means "a coming," and for Christian people it is a time of looking forward to the coming of Christ. Advent is the period of time we do all those things that get us ready to celebrate Christ's day of birth. We put up trees and other decorations, wrap gifts, bake cookies and fruitcakes, write out cards for friends, start humming carols.

While we are doing all these things, it is important to remember that Jesus Christ is the cause of all the excitement. So during

Advent, think about long ago — what it was like when Christ was born; think about today — how it makes a difference to us that he was born; and think about some tomorrow — when Christ will surprise us by coming again.

Today we light the first candle on the Advent wreath. Each week we will be lighting an additional candle to indicate that with the coming of Christ, things get brighter.

[Light candle]

O God, we rejoice that you are coming to be with us. Over the next few weeks we will prepare to welcome you. During that time, help us to treat one another with the same loving kindness we would offer to the Christchild. Perhaps we can be as candles: bright for you, warm toward others, lighting your way to come among us. We wait eagerly as we pray in Jesus' name. Amen.

Second Sunday
[Light two candles]

O God, in lighting these candles we give thanks that Jesus brings an illuminating hope into the world. Because of him, we believe that good is stronger than evil. Help us to do good deeds, to be a people of hope, to let our faith shine forth. In Jesus' name, Amen.

Third Sunday
[Light three candles, including rose candle]

O God, with the lighting of these candles may we, too, be set aglow with the bright joy that comes with being touched by your Spirit. As these candles melt down and Advent days melt away, may the warmth of the season grow into a glad greeting for the Child of Christmas. We celebrate life and we offer our prayer in that Child's name. Amen.

Fourth Sunday
Today we light four Advent candles. Only the Christ candle, central in the wreath as Christ is central in our lives, remains to be kindled. The day of the Messiah's birth draws nearer. In lighting the candles, we brighten the way for the coming of Christ among us. We welcome the humble Child born to be our Savior.

[Light four candles]

O God, we feel an excitement and expectancy in our spirits, for Christmas Day will soon be here. Though the glow of candles is but a flicker, your presence in our midst sets us aflame with a bold and energetic love. Where darkness resides, may your light find its home. In Jesus' name we pray. Amen.

❈

Christmas Day

O God, we join together in prayer this morning asking that the Spirit of Christmas dwell in us according to our need.

Where there is pain or despondency, may the Spirit come with brightness and may the touch of the Child be one of healing.

Where there is aimlessness, may the Spirit be as a star giving direction and urging us on.

Where belief is scant and faith weak, may the Spirit take us to the manger where we have our surprising beginnings as believers and people of faith.

Where selfishness exists, may the Spirit grant us that wisdom of the Magi, a wisdom that enables us to give with generosity and more, with an attitude of worship.

Where values are confused, may the Spirit of Christmas set them aright, for in this season we celebrate that which is most valuable…the opportunity to offer you glory and praise, the chance to affirm an inclusive and holy sense of family, the knowledge that your peace can be our way in the world.

We pray in the name of the Christmas Child. Amen.

❈

Christmas Pageant

Call to Worship

We are here today, and we are excited today, because we have a story to share. It is a story about long ago and far away. It is filled with angels and shepherds and travelers from afar. But it is also a story for here and now because it tells about a baby, parents, friends, animals and – most of all – about how much God loves us. Quite a story, this Christmas story… whenever we hear it or tell it, we get excited by what it says. And that is surely the way it should be.

Prayer

O God, you surprise us with the birth of Jesus, your loving way of coming among us. You amaze us with the life and work and play of Jesus, your loving way of identifying with us. So bless us now as we share the story of Jesus with one another through the Christmas pageant. It is our way of saying thank you for the gift of Christmas itself. We ask that you fill us with your Spirit as we pray in the name of your Child. Amen.

❄

Church Annual Meeting

O God, on this day of our annual meeting, we give thanks for your presence and support and guidance, for in these we find our strength. By your grace and through the committed efforts of church members, much has been accomplished over the past twelve months...perhaps more than seemed possible at our meeting a year ago. We pray that our satisfactions become motivations for time ahead, that our growth in number/spirit be sign and symbol of developing faith.

We offer special thanks today for the service of persons who have completed terms as officers or committee members; may they sense the appreciation we extend through you to them. And we give thanks for the service of those whose terms are new or continuing; grant them vision and energy and a spirit of joyful cooperation.

Build us as the church. Use us as living stones. We pray in the name of Jesus Christ, the cornerstone of our faith. Amen.

Church Annual Meeting (before meal)

O God, we have set the time, prepared the food, designed the agenda, but it is you who gathers us together as a church. Help us today to be your church at its finest. May our friendship be fond, may our conversation be creative, may our decisions bear witness to your presence in our midst and to your promise for our future. We trust that your Spirit will guide us always toward being a church of committed and compassionate disciples in service to the One in whose name we pray. Amen.

✽

Family Sunday

Loving God, we offer our prayer this day for families.

We ask that there be occasions for celebrating connectedness, for healing brokenness, for discovering ways of becoming closer even as geographical distances and difficult issues sometimes work to keep family members apart.

We seek your guidance for parents as they struggle to affirm wholesome principles in a world of skewed values and scary problems, as they strive to show and share what matters in a world of "whatever" attitudes.

We pray your presence every moment in the lives of children. Be their protector and source of wisdom, a power permitting them to slow the pace in a race toward adulthood and allowing them to linger in the spiritually productive environs of childhood.

We look to you as the catalyst enabling productive intergenerational interaction, encouraging young and old to learn from one another in an atmosphere of mutual respect.

Grace us with your Spirit. And strengthen families as instruments of doing your will and extending your love. We pray in Jesus' name. Amen.

✽

A Sharing of Burdens, Sins, Griefs and Guilts
(especially for Maundy Thursday)

In the pews (or seats), you will find blank pieces of paper. Please take one and write upon it something you feel as a burden, a sin, a grief or a guilt within your life. These will be things that are in some way killing you, preventing you from living life freely and fully. In writing and offering them anonymously, you are asking that the power of God come to bear upon them – perhaps to bring light and life where death and darkness seem to be at work. What grieves or burdens you? What oppresses you as sin or guilt? Write, and make these things your offerings in Jesus' name.

✳

Memorial Day
(at cemetery)

Gracious God, on this Memorial Day, we recall with fondness and acknowledge with gratitude sacrifices made on behalf of others. We honor persons who gave their lives in acting to preserve the principles and the people they cherished. May our recollections lead us to continuing thankfulness as well as to a renewing of our personal dedication to forms of service that foster justice and liberty, reconciliation and peace.

On this day of reflection, help us to remember the sacrificial love of Jesus Christ and to recognize that his style of service focused intently upon the deepest needs of humankind. Grant that we may, in good faith, have the courage to address issues, to extend our talents, to devote our attention in a manner that helps build a better world for the entire human family.

Our memories this day have faces, and we know that each face we recall is that of one of your beloved children. For the gift of their lives we offer deep and respectful thanks. In Jesus' name, Amen.

✳

Memorial Day

Loving God, on this Memorial Day weekend we pray for peace. Through our appreciative remembrance of persons known and unknown, may we resolve to work for a world that no longer tolerates making casualties of your children. This day we confess our longing for a future in which parents can raise children with confidence that the rumblings of war will be replaced by the triumphant song of life. To the people in places where conflicts now smolder or rage, convey your comfort and hope, and turn the energy that goes into sustaining a war toward the task of making peace.

We pray for peace in this nation. Violence thrives in many forms of abuse. Racial and other interpersonal tensions abound as we fall prey to our prejudices and succumb to stereotyping. The gap between rich and poor widens into a chasm. Our society's refugees, the homeless, populate streets and shelters. Drugs deal death throughout the population. Fill us with a dedication to make changes, to stand with Spirit for reconciliation and renewal, to risk following Christ as witnesses to your will and ways.

We pray for peace within families and within ourselves. Where home is more a battleground than a haven, where the fabric of family life is frayed, where abuse goes unconfronted, enter in, O God, with your power of healing. And, also, do come into the interior places of our lives where struggles abound and where tangled emotions cause the battle fatigue we know as stress. Help us to use a spiritual eraser on our list of personal enemies and to build friendships as an act of faith.

We pray in the name of Jesus Christ, Teacher of the ways of peace. Amen.

✻

Baccalaureate

Call to Worship

Leader: It takes all kinds of courses to form a curriculum, to open our minds and to extend our knowledge.

People: We give thanks this day for our learning.

Leader: It takes all kinds of music to sing humanity's song – rap and rock, classical and country, blues and folk.

People: We give thanks this day for our singing.

Leader: It takes all kinds of people to create a school environment, to build a community, to inhabit a varied and wonderful world.

People: We give thanks this day for all who are our brothers and sisters.

Leader: It takes all kinds of skills to keep a team playing, to keep a business booming, to keep a family thriving, to keep our spirits growing.

People: We give thanks this day for our talents.

Leader: It takes all kinds of dreams to turn ideas into progress, to shape a future filled with joy and peace.

People: We give thanks today for our hopes.

All: How good to join together in a spirit of unity and gratitude.

❦

Confirmation

The following prayers are specific to certain confirmands. They provide examples of prayers that might be offered on the occasion of confirmation.

_____, child of God, may God use your humor and happiness to bring healing into the lives of persons around you. May you accept from God the gift of a life balanced between effort and relaxation. And may you find that your talents for art and music can become offerings to others, ways of fulfilling your mission in this world, ways of honoring your Maker.

_____, child of God, may our Creator be your partner in times of fun and happiness, your trusted advisor when you need help or guidance. May the energy and aggressiveness and drive you bring to athletics serve you spiritually as well, helping you accomplish great things in this world. And may these things prove both satisfying to you and of service to others.

_____, child of God, may the Lord who has blessed you with a keen mind guide you to use it well for the benefit of many. May your sense of humor and athletic skills always provide you with a balance to the serious and stressful sides of life. And may divine grace supply you with understandings of prayer that will shape your ways of serving God with gladness.

_____, child of God, may God open up for you adventures that will help you discover an ever-deepening faith. May all worries or annoyances become opportunities for God to reveal a steadfast, healing, enlivening love. And may you realize fully the beauty that shines upon others through your outgoing nature.

_____, child of God, may our Creator nurture your optimistic outlook on life, your natural inclination toward friendliness and kindness. May you find constant companionship with Christ through times of trial and triumph, growing in faith as you experience that steadfast presence. And may your music always bear witness to a light and thriving spirit.

_____, child of God, may our Source and Sustainer enhance your ability to set goals and to achieve them, to surround yourself with positive and supportive friends. May your faith help you find clarity amidst complexity, joyfulness throughout life's ups and downs. And may your attachment to God grow as your spirit matures through the years and as you find a home within the church.

_____, child of God, may our Maker speak to you lifelong through the wonders of the natural world and work with your ability to perform in ways that touch the lives of others. May you discover a comfort within time and a faith that encourages you to bold inquiry and steady growth. May the Word of God speak strongly through your words and actions.

_____, child of God, may our Creator direct your energy and spunkiness in ways that lead to success, while tempering any impatience with the wisdom of faith. May the Spirit be as the wind in your sails as you move through life. And may your poise, your verbal skills, and your talents be used to bring joy to others and glory to God.

_____, child of God, may our Maker and Redeemer guide the growth of your faith. Grant that the bright energy and spiritual intuition that fills you lead to enjoyment, satisfaction, and deep recognition of companionship with Jesus Christ.

_____, child of God, we ask that your spiritual curiosity permits you to probe deeply into the issues of faith. May your searching maintain a natural balance of self-assurance and graciousness.

Note: Prayers/blessings offered at confirmation need to be person-specific. My hope is that the examples provided inspire the creation of meaningful confirmation liturgy.

International Peace Day

Loving God, help us to be like Jesus in our relationships with others, in our approach to issues and events, in our sense of your presence. Equip us with a love so powerful that we become, above all else, fervent peace-makers in a world prone to reliance upon violence. Teach us the skills necessary to quiet our spirits when they are troubled or anxious or raging with anger. Give us, by the power of your Spirit, the ability to construct bridges and to find common ground between persons at odds with one another. Engage us in the discipline of serious prayer for victims of violence whether they dwell in a nation at war within itself or fall to oppression from afar, whether they play in a local schoolyard or live in fear next door.

Remind us daily of Jesus' reconciling ways, of his passion for compassion, and of his message that your realm is right in our midst. Grant us the will and the wisdom to discern it. Continuing our prayer, we offer it in Jesus' name and in the words he taught us saying... [the prayer of Jesus]. Amen.

Start of School

Call to Worship

Leader: To everything a season,

People: And a time to every purpose under heaven.

Leader: Time for relaxed summer sojourns and for scheduled daily school bus rides,

People: For involvement with recreational activities and for immersion in challenging studies.

Leader: Time for setting a solid career course and for veering off in new directions,

People: For establishing firm friendships and for discovering the solace of solitude.

Leader: Time for focusing on wondrous potential and for honestly accepting limits,

People: For appreciating the moment at hand and for contemplating eternity.

All: In all circumstances and through all seasons, we offer our thanks and praise to God.

Prayer

We offer our prayer this morning, O God, for persons who have returned or soon will return to school...for teachers, students, administrators, and support staff.

Fill all those who work at schools with a sense of purpose and high calling. Allow them to feel the genuine collegiality that helps form and sustain an environment for learning. Keep alive in teachers an intellectual curiosity that is never self-centered...let there be eagerness to share, openness in dialogue, excitement at discovery and insight.

Charge all students with an energy to be scholars. Grant them a willingness to work that stretches abilities and challenges minds toward thinking that is critical, keen and creative. Nurture an appreciation for the opportunity to learn.

Remind us, we pray, of the ongoing task of faith, one that is in fact the coursework of our entire lives...to seek to know your will, to do it with compassion, to share it with joy.

We offer this prayer in the name of Jesus Christ. Amen.

✤

Prayer for Those Affected by Natural Disaster and Ongoing Deprivation/Oppression

Loving God, we offer our prayer this morning for those whose lives have been torn by the affects of storm. For the people of _____, we ask that your Spirit renew and comfort them, that the generosity of persons seeking to help be channeled in ways that promote healing.

We offer our prayer for those whose lives have been scattered by storms of battles. There are places where firefights make silence uncommon, where the whims or policies of governing regimes reign terror sporadically and brutally. Extend your peace and establish your calm, we pray.

We offer our prayer, too, for those whose lives have been rent by battles with hunger or hopelessness. Grant us responsiveness to the needs of refugees in [name countries or reasons]. Whenever the pangs of hunger and the pains of starvation call out, whenever the hopelessness of having no home and the horror of having no hope come before us, charge us with a responsive compassion.

Keep us in prayer, guide us in action, in the name of Jesus Christ. Amen.

❧

CROP Walk

Loving God, on this day of the Church World Service CROP Walk, we acknowledge the generosity of sponsors and we ask that you bless all participants with a safe journey and a spirit of enthusiasm. Hear our prayer also for the hungry of the Earth. We are grateful that you are a generous and caring Provider, that you intend for all persons to live in good health, to have equal access to the bounty and beauty of creation, to have sufficient nourishment for proper growth and development. We regret that hunger persists for millions in your family, and we confess that many who practice greed and waste and luxurious consumption resist making changes in behavior and deny that their practices offend you. Equip us, we pray, to be instruments of change, co-creators with you of a world more whole and just. May that world be one in which all people dine at one table, in which resources are well used to the benefit of all, in which hunger itself dies with the birth of full and compassionate outreach.

We remember today, also, those who hunger for healing in body and spirit, those who hunger for clarity in relationships and processes of decision-making, those who hunger for justice and peace amidst situations of oppression or conflict. For these people we now offer our silent prayer... [Silence]

We pray in the name of Jesus Christ who meets the hunger of our needs with the sustenance of your Spirit, who bids us pray together saying... [the prayer of Jesus]. Amen.

❈

World Communion

O God, our prayer as a congregation is a simple one. We ask that on this World Communion Sunday we focus our faith on the Christ whose sovereignty is expressed through the hospitality found at table. Draw us toward you in quiet, steadfast ways.

In remembering you, we sense the opportunity to serve others.

In recognizing your presence, we come to know ourselves.

God of healing and hopefulness, grace and goodness, hear our prayer offered in the name of Jesus Christ. Amen.

❈

Stewardship Service / Commissioning

Loving God, by your grace we have been given the task of shepherding our brothers and sisters along the path of stewardship. Grant us the vigilance, concern and love that will enable us to turn our task into a pilgrimage of faith. Let your Spirit move within us so that we might move others.

Through our work of tending, help us to become skillful in nurturing a sense of generosity, feeding a desire to grow in servanthood, encouraging a hope for progressive development in faith. We pray in the name of our Good Shepherd and Savior. Amen.

❈

A Wedding Blessing

Loving God, Creator of all that is good, we ask your blessing upon (names)_____and_____, upon the union of their spirits and upon the course of their lives together.

We pray that they be good *for* one another, that they encourage the development of individual gifts even as they experience the joys of shared pleasures. Keep them alert to the ways they complement, gain strength, and learn from each other.

We pray that they be good *to* one another, that they lavish time upon the relationship, letting it grow in an environment of mutual trust, expressed appreciation, and caring attentiveness. In a world of plentiful stress and high demands, grant to (names)_____ and_____ the deep understanding of each other's needs, an understanding that can become a reliable source of healing.

We pray that they be good *with* one another, that they continue through the years to share the delights of time at table, adventures in the outdoors, engaging and challenging conversation, gentle touches, moments of inspiration. Enable (names)_____ and_____to sense the synergy of their partnership, to be ever-grateful for their opportunity to be together. And we especially ask that the lightness of love fill their days, that there be much laughter in their future, much joy as only you can give.

Creator of life, God of grace and good news, we rejoice in this marriage and in the wonder of your love that embraces us all. We offer this prayer in the name of Jesus Christ. Amen.

❧

Blessing of an Adoptive Child

God of joy and God of peace, we ask that the new life of (name)_____ become a long life rich in valued relationships, abundant in adventure, full in faith. Grant to (name)_____ a discerning and gracious spirit.

Bless (name)_____ with contentment in good measure, patience through difficult times, appreciation of opportunities provided, attentiveness to personal gifts, generosity toward others, and wisdom blended with kindness. May this child truly be your child. We offer our prayer in the name of Jesus Christ. Amen.

❧

Habitat House Dedication Prayer

Gracious God, Creator of all that is, we give thanks that your love provides the foundation of our work together, that your Spirit guides all constructive efforts to embody love in deeds. This day we lift up our eyes and we see a Habitat home; grant us the wisdom to recognize it as a reminder of the psalmist who lifted his eyes to the hills and received the sure message that you are the sole source of humanity's help and hope.

As we dedicate this house to you, we ask your blessing upon donators of land and labor, contributors of materials and time, raisers of funds and awareness. You have called us to pound in nails and pound out policies; you have taken a body of dreamers and shaped it into an extended and extensive family of faith. For your patient nurture and support we are deeply grateful. Now we ask that you bless the (name)_____ family as they take up residence in this place and in this community. May the Spirit dwell within these good people as they inhabit their home.

We offer our prayer in the name of One who was both skilled carpenter and saving Christ. Amen.

✵

World AIDS Day

Loving God, we come together this day because you do not want us to be distant from one another and because we have much for which to be thankful.

Though many of us come with sorrows at the loss of friends, partners or relatives, we are grateful that the AIDS virus is not victorious even as it claims new victims. Through the courage of those affected by it, the commitment of those who devote their research to its downfall, the compassion of those who care for the stricken, its vanquishing is sure.

Help us to fight boldly against the more insidious aspects of the disease: a fear that sometimes isolates victims, a prejudice that condemns them, an ignorance unhealthy to us all. Move us to greater compassion, to tender attentiveness, to growing understanding.

As we cherish the memories of those who have died, equip us to hold fast to the hope that more will live. Remind us daily that even the most virulent virus is no match for a vital and tenacious love. Grant us grace in our living, and urge us to make every moment of every day an acclamation of life.

In our Savior's name we pray. Amen.

❉

Dedication of Memorial Plaque
(or book containing planned gifts)

Loving God, we dedicate this plaque (book) today in remembrance of those whose bequests have strengthened this congregation's ability to build a ministry and to sustain its buildings and grounds. We dedicate it also in recognition of the generosity of all who plan their giving in ways that create new possibilities for faithful action in the future. There is, we believe, no finer way to give thanks for life itself than through gifts that increase the vitality and the health of the body of Christ called your church. With gratitude and with hope, we dedicate this memorial plaque (book). In the name of Jesus Christ, Amen.

❉

Prayer at a Workshop for the Developmentally Disabled

O God, you have created all persons and blessed us with a range of gifts, with different ways of seeing the world. Grant us deep pleasure at the variety which enriches humankind and fill us with joy at the contacts which bring us understanding of one another.

We give thanks for the opportunities found in this place – to be creative, to be productive, to find support and companionship and friendship. Open our eyes to the good work done here, the lives fulfilled here, the relationships formed here, the hopes made whole here. In a spirit of gratitude we pray. Amen.

❀

A Prayer for Quilters

Gracious God, as we design, arrange and assemble from many pieces the quilts that are products of our own abilities and dedication, we remember your creative activity in this world.

We are grateful for your creation of a planet varied in color and texture, for your design of humanity as a crazy-quilt of races and cultures.

We appreciate as individuals the way your Spirit works to stitch together the pieces of our lives, to do so with the kind of loving care that goes into making the most beautiful of quilts.

We acknowledge your ultimate skill as Maker and Shaper of everything that is good. And we ask that you use all the work of our hands, all the exercise of our talents, all the joy in our hearts to do what is pleasing in your sight.

We pray in the name of Jesus Christ, Craftsman and Teacher, Redeemer and Friend. Amen.

Benedictions

I once had a neighbor who never said, "hello," or, "how are you," or, "what's up," or "what's happening." His customary greeting was this: "What's the good news?" I hasten to note that this fellow was not a particularly religious person who expected a proclamation of gospel to greet his question. What he hoped for was something positive (a universal human longing not confined to my neighborhood) and something that would cheer him on his way.

Benedictions – "good sayings" – are precisely what my neighbor was looking for. They are absolutely what we all need at the close of worship. Benedictions remind us of God's gracious ever-presence, assure us of God's timely/timeless love, charge us with the calling to be God's people in this world.

That's the good news!

Through this season of Advent,
  may our faith grow from flicker to flame,
  our hope from glimmer to glow.
And may our love for God and neighbor
  be brave and bold and bright. Amen.

✣ Advent
✣ Faith, fire of
✣ God, love of

𝒦eep your spirits bright with eagerness.
Feel the power of wonder poised for joy.
Wait in hope. And prepare a welcoming way for the One who
    comes to be with us. Amen.

  ✣ Advent
  ✣ Incarnation
  ✣ Faith, brightness of

𝒫romised God's presence, let the hopefulness of Advent fill us
and inspire us to live our faith as an adventure. Now, the peace of
Christ be among us all. Amen.

  ✣ Advent
  ✣ God, presence of
  ✣ Hope

𝒜s the Word became flesh,
    May our faith become deed.
And may the love of God
    Animate this body of believers
So that through worship and service
    We distribute the bread of compassion and
    the cup of new life. Amen.

  ✣ Advent
  ✣ Communion
  ✣ Incarnation

𝒞arry your faith as you would carry the Christ child,
    With openness, care and joy.
And work in good faith to make this world
    A home fit for every child given birth,
    A place with food, fairness and peace available to all.
Give thanks and rejoice. God is with us. Amen.

  ✣ Advent
  ✣ Incarnation
  ✣ Faith, activity/activities of

Watch for the One whose life lightens the darkness,
  the One whose presence makes vital the good news.
Rejoice in his advent. Respond to his call. Serve no other.
  Amen.

❖ Advent
❖ Jesus, service to
❖ God

In the silence of night, hear the cry of a newborn babe.
Dark world, receive your Light.
Bright hope, rejoice in a Savior. Amen.

❖ Christmas Eve (candlelight service)
❖ Light
❖ Salvation

In the silence of the night our praise finds its voice.
In the birth of a Savior our hopes come to life.
May the joy of Christmas fill our spirits and give form
  to our faith. Amen.

❖ Christmas Eve (candlelight service)
❖ Hope
❖ Incarnation

Within the silence of this night, sense the majesty of God.
Within the holiness of this night, discern the living Christ.
  Praise God with your devotion.
  Adore Christ with your service.
  Live a joyful faith. Amen.

❖ Christmas Eve
❖ Faith, components of
❖ God, presence of

*T*hrough the coming of a Child,
God infuses the world with a holy presence.
Receive this gift of Christmas,
And live by grace to love in Christ's name. Amen.

❖ Christmas
❖ Incarnation
❖ Faith, living

*I*f you have ever dreamed of time redeemed, receive it as God's gift in the coming year.

Pursue faithfulness. Renew your love for God and neighbor. Do what is good and just in the name of Jesus Christ. Amen.

❖ New Year
❖ Time
❖ Faithfulness

*R*esist evil and rely on the love of God. Develop compassion and determine to follow the teachings of Christ. Practice faith and pray for the guidance of the Holy Spirit.

May peace dwell in our midst and live through our deeds. Amen.

❖ Trinity
❖ Faith, practice of
❖ Peace

*I*n the commonplace, discern the holy. In the context of Christian community, find fellowship. In this church, grow through service. In Christ, root your faith and your lives. God be with us and within us. Amen.

❖ Common life
❖ Community
❖ Faithfulness

May the goodness of God guide us to do what is loving and right. May the sovereignty of Christ prompt us to discern and follow the ways of faithfulness. May the holiness of the Spirit inspire our work for justice and peace. Amen.

✤ Trinity
✤ Faith, living
✤ Discipleship

These are the true resources for our faith: Perceived needs and acknowledged abilities, enduring hope and motivating love. Use them as best you can to honor God and to serve your neighbor. Amen.

✤ Faith, resources of
✤ Faithfulness
✤ Discipleship

In contemplation, find contentment. In service to others, find satisfaction for your spirits.

In the privacy of penitential prayer, discover the power of divine forgiveness. Live in God's grace; live out God's love. Amen.

✤ Ash Wednesday
✤ Faith, practice of
✤ Grace

Beyond this day of waving palms let there be the outreach of welcoming spirits. Open yourselves to the living presence of Christ. Get into the faith with all your heart and mind and strength. Amen.

✤ Palm Sunday
✤ Faith, living
✤ Commitment

Hear the good news: The tomb is empty and the world is filled with the love of God. Let your hearts rejoice and your spirits soar. Celebrate life in the name of the risen Christ! Alleluia and Amen.

✤ Easter
✤ Joy
✤ God, love of

Rejoice! Be glad! You are freed to serve God, to live in peace. Celebrate life in the name of the risen Christ. Amen.

❖ Easter
❖ Joy
❖ Resurrection, impact of

Face up to the costs and joys of your faith. As you come face-to-face with the problems that beset this planet, the needs that affect your neighbors, and the struggles and strivings that challenge your spirits, serve well the Christ who calls you. Amen.

❖ Faithfulness
❖ Justice
❖ Mission

By the grace of God, for the love of Christ, in the power of the Spirit – rejoice! Live life lightly for the miracle it is. Amen.

❖ Trinity
❖ Joy
❖ Faith, living

In days to come…listen to the Christ whose words tell of the world where God wills us to live. Follow the Spirit whose guidance turns our wanderings into a pilgrimage of faith. And pray that God always comes between us so we might be drawn closer together in love. May the peace of Christ fill us. Amen.

❖ God, realm of
❖ Trinity
❖ Faith, journey of

May your lives be transformed by God's forgiveness and grace; may your actions be informed by the wisdom of Word and Spirit. And may the love of Christ be at the heart of all you do. Amen.

❖ God, love of
❖ Transformation
❖ Grace

Adhere to the will of God and you will bond with others in the family of faith. Follow in the steps of Jesus and you will find the way of love and peace. Move as the Spirit leads and you will enjoy life's finest freedom. Amen.

✤ Faith, living
✤ Trinity
✤ God, will of

Recognize the resurrected Christ; as you live for him he lives in you. And for the least of the Earth, do the most that you can. As we embrace our neighbors, we reach in love toward God.
Peace be within and among us. Amen.

✤ Mission
✤ Peace
✤ Faith, living

Let us go now to be alert and alive for the sake of our God. Receive the Word of hope. Speak the Word of truth. And may the Spirit of God be enfleshed in us as we spread the good Word of a love divine. Amen.

✤ God, Word of
✤ God, love of
✤ Faith, living

May the Word of God speak anew through the language of caring deeds; through the signs of hope within a troubled world; and through the understandings that come to receptive hearts.
Peace be within and among us. Amen.

✤ God, Word of
✤ Faith, characteristics of
✤ Peace

Bless us now, O God, with the spiritual poise to be positive about our faith in all circumstances and situations. Fill us with the strength to love, the courage to exercise compassion, the boldness to seek justice, the wisdom to trust gentleness. Let us honor the living Christ in all we do. Amen.

❖ Faith, strength of
❖ Mission
❖ God, love of

May all our thoughts, words, and deeds create a patchwork pattern of blessings; a sketch of the Spirit's movement; a moving picture of Christ's love; a design for building up God's realm in our midst. Amen.

❖ Faith, creativity of
❖ God, realm of
❖ Trinity

May the practice of faith define the person you are. And may the love of God shape the person you will become. Now and always, serve God with gladness. Amen.

❖ Faith, practice of
❖ Future
❖ God, love of

May we hear the clarity of God's Word amidst the noises of the world. May the living Christ speak to us and through us in everything we do or say. And may we commune with the Spirit of truth, letting it expand our understandings and extend our faith. Amen.

❖ Mission
❖ Faith, growth of
❖ God, Word of

And now may our Creator touch our lives with a Spirit that will support an honest consideration of weaknesses, a courageous confrontation of fears, a creative formation of hopes, a joyous love of God. Peace be among us and within us. Amen.

❖ Hope
❖ Joy
❖ Fears

God remain with us, in us, and among us. So grow in Christ to fullness; go with one another in peace. Amen.

❖ General
❖ God, presence of
❖ Faith, fullness of

May a spirit of determination guide you toward the destination of life anew. May your days be filled with deeds just and good, and be blessed with an awareness of God's steadfast love. Amen.

❖ God, steadfast love of
❖ Faith, journey of
❖ Life, newness of

May the sowing of good seed lead to the growing of sturdy belief. Allow the Word to sink in, the Spirit to nourish, the Christ to tend. And by the grace of God, may faith flourish. Amen.

❖ Faith, seeds of
❖ Faith, growth of
❖ God, presence of

Let nothing inhibit the enactment of your faith, for you are inhabited by the Spirit of God. Entertain high hopes about everything good, for these coincide with the will of God. And treat with high regard all persons you meet, for they are brothers and sisters in the family of God. Go in peace. Amen.

❖ Faith, practice of
❖ Hope
❖ Mission

When we are fired up to act in good faith, we reduce hatred to ashes, and we wield the restorative power of upbuilding love. May all that we do be inspired by the God who is our Creator, Sustainer and Enabler. Amen.

❖ Healing
❖ Love, power of
❖ Faith, activity/activities of

Let the needs of those you meet be your call to faithful action. Let the deeds of your life be worthy of the name of Christ. Respond in love. Renew through prayer. Rely upon God. Amen.

+ Faith, activity/activities of
+ Mission
+ Discipleship

Our God is the renewer of covenants, the restorer of souls, the redeemer of all creation. Receive God's love and relay it to others through word and deed. Amen.

+ God, nature of
+ God, love of
+ Discipleship

In days ahead, trust in God to watch between us, to dwell within us, to move among us as an empowering Spirit of love and truth. Amen.

+ God, trust in
+ God, presence of
+ Faithfulness

Let us go with thanks in our hearts for God's good gift of lifetime. Keep companionship with the Spirit eternal and close contact with the One who was and is and ever shall be our loving, living Savior. Amen.

+ Christ, closeness to
+ Time
+ Thankfulness

Though bread and cup get cleared away, the Spirit dwells within. Live each day as a table grace: Remain in communion with Christ and with one another. Extend yourselves to serve. Give thanks always. Amen.

+ Communion
+ Grace
+ Faith, living

Each and every day, honor the person of Jesus by studying the character of his faith and by practicing the wisdom of his ways. As the Spirit empowers you, enact the Good News and make a difference in the world. Amen.

❧ Faithfulness
❧ Faith, activity/activities of
❧ Mission

To every hope that is humble and holy, offer your spirit as a home. To every deed that is good and just, extend a strong helping hand. Let Christ dwell within you and your faith will thrive. Amen.

❧ Faith, activity/activities of
❧ Faith, living
❧ Mission

As the ways of Christ inspire us, as attunement to the Spirit empowers us, we note with joy God's love alive in our midst. May all we do and say bring out the best of our service and ring out the Good News of our faith. Amen.

❧ God, love of
❧ Service
❧ Faithfulness

Be guided by God toward the expansion and extension of faith as the Spirit graces you with power; practice daily discipleship. And in response to the love of Christ, simply serve. Amen.

❧ Faith, growth of
❧ Discipleship
❧ Service

May God shape our actions so that every deed issues forth as witness to a healing and holy love. May God give form to our faith so we live with confidence and hope, creativity and grace. Amen.

❧ Healing
❧ Faith, form of
❧ Faith, living

*T*he bread is broken, the cup is shared. And all who partake are no longer worlds apart but rather united in Christ. Sense the grace, feel the peace, live the faith. Amen.

❧ World Communion
❧ Unity
❧ Inclusiveness

*A*s children of the living God, get into the world as the Spirit gets into you…with invigorating hope and courageous witness and transforming love. Peace be among us and within us now and always. Amen.

❧ God, children of
❧ Mission
❧ Faith, activity/activities of

*M*ay a purity of spirit and a devotion to Christ ignite your desire to build a world more humane and holy. And may a regard for the dignity of all and a passion for enacting the love of God sustain and support your efforts to serve. Amen.

❧ Devotion
❧ Justice
❧ Inclusiveness

*E*njoy every moment in God's good creation. Treasure time. Savor every opportunity to serve in Christ's name. Treasure others. Follow every movement of the Spirit's leading. Treasure faith. And in all things, give thanks. Amen.

❧ Life, appreciation for
❧ Thankfulness
❧ Discipleship

*S*hare the love of God. Place your hope in Christ. Be open to the Spirit. And may your days be graced with joy. Amen.

❧ Trinity
❧ Hope
❧ Joy

Resist what is wrong. Guard what is good. Spend your lives wisely, supporting with a generous outpouring of Christly love and discernment:

✢ values faith values,

✢ actions the Spirit activates,

✢ grace that God grants. Amen.

✤ Justice

✤ Faith, activity/activities of

✤ Discipleship

Let us go now to serve God through our words and deeds. May grace, mercy and peace nourish us to live as thanks-givers. Amen.

✤ Thanksgiving

✤ Faith, nourishment of

✤ Service

PARABLES

As a spiritual leader, Jesus was known as rabbi-teacher. He did not gain his reputation for wisdom by producing vast volumes of theological writings. He did not proclaim the good news primarily through preaching. Instead, he let his actions speak. And he told stories.

Jesus' characteristic way of conveying his message was through sharing parables. These pithy little stories about common life, ordinary events or easily understood situations demanded careful listening of those who heard them. They also invited some decision-making in response to questions the parables tended to provoke. Questions such as: What on earth is Jesus trying to get across? Why does this story make me uneasy? What is it saying about God? What is it saying about God's relationship with me?

What makes the parables so alluring is that they teach by indirection. They acknowledge that spiritual truth is not something acquired by rote. Parables do not ask for acceptance of data; they do ask for engagement with ideas. Jesus likely chose the telling of parables as his teaching technique because it revealed the cooperative nature of faith development. It is when God and listeners work (and play) together that the meanings of parables emerge.

Parables invite ongoing discussion. In that, they are building blocks of the faith community. They encourage dialogue, for parables do not have one correct interpretation but rather suggest multiple levels of meaning. One can easily imagine the disciples and others in Jesus' audiences having long conversations about the parables they heard…. Have you ever felt like that elder brother? What do you think of that woman who wore down the judge? What's the pearl of great price in your life? Did you ever get treated like those laborers who got hired last?

Part of the appeal of parables is that they are not overtly religious in subject or tone. Although the parables assume that listeners have a basic knowledge of religious and cultural traditions or norms, the stories themselves are anything but preachy. Jesus used them to reach everybody, not just a select spiritual in-crowd.

The parables I offer have a variety of settings and styles and principle characters. Some of them have in-church settings. These I include because church involvement is part of our common life experience, and I suspect this is especially true for purchasers of this book. Other parables I include seem unrelated to anything approximating a religious setting. These focus on such normal activities as shopping, a child's play, and observing a scene in the city. I hope that none of the parables presents a message that comes across as either too obvious or too obscure. And I certainly hope they provoke questions and open conversations and nurture personal reflection.

*A personal note...*A good number of these parables have their theme and setting associated with food and/or with communion-related situations. This is an intentional choice. On the one hand, culinary concentration reflects my own love of cooking and of all things edible. But there is a broader reason for my choice. In a world where norms and traditions get homogenized out of existence or are grossly misunderstood across cultural lines, recognizing our shared need to obtain, prepare, and eat food seems a promising place to start in affirming our common humanity. Though tastes and manners may differ among us, it is a basic act of caring to practice table hospitality. I believe it was an example of Jesus' genius to "put himself" into a meal. Every time we celebrate Holy Communion, we truly participate in an enacted parable. And World Communion, the occasion of sacramental connection throughout the Earth, is to my mind a genuine miracle of "union with Christ and with one another" (words of the liturgy I use).

If these parables have been well-prepared, they will provide a spiritual fare that gives you something to chew on and to savor. And they will give you a taste of the grace and the love of God.

[This section of the book begins and concludes with brief "poetic parables," items meant to encourage you to consider "genres within the genre" as you create parables of your own. The contexts of these

two pieces are city and farm...my way of affirming again that wherever we are, God is.]

·❀·

A Token Congregation

*T*he benches are hard.
The windows reveal no outside world, only the stations.
The people, for the most part, remain unspeaking.
It is a strange subterranean silence full of sound that sways
    the people...
the bass run rumbles of wheels
the descant screeched by a choir of brakes
the mumbled litany of connections and destinations.
There is movement of flesh and blood,
A press of hip to hip, of seated shoulder to standing thigh.
This journey together of intimate strangers,
    perhaps no holy thing, is yet the commuters' cramped
    communion.

·❀·

A Gift Clumsily Given

*H*e lived a tattered existence on the streets of New York City.
She lived in a luxury apartment on Central Park East. He knew the
city from its innards out, from underground up, and could tell you
which subways gave the longest ride to those who used them as
sleepers. She knew the city as a stranger for her doorman and security system to keep outside, and her limousine had heavy curtains
that marooned her in the back seat. He stood on Fifth Avenue outside the window of Steuben Glass holding in his mittened hands the
shopping bag containing all accumulated worldly possessions. She
stood inside the store cooing like a pigeon and fingering crystal
objects that cost more than he could panhandle in a year.

The street and its people were dressed for Christmas. Lampposts
and signs wore greens while those who walked uptown and down
sported corsages and pinkish faces wreathed with scarves or roundish
winter hats. The haste was more cheerful than frantic. Store window
displays in Saks, Bloomingdale's and F.A.O. Schwarz arrested

passersby with fairyland scenes and tiny figures that moved as though
alive. In the streets, the grey-black slush shifted beneath the tires of
the traffic and the feet of hordes of shoppers. It bore no resemblance
to the fluffy, dazzling, pristine white snow in the store displays. Blue-
uniformed Salvation Army attendants stood staunchly by their red
tripods set up beside the bus stops and subway entrances and news
stands where people would already be reaching for money or tokens.
Just off the Avenue on Fifty-Seventh Street across from Tiffany's, a
wool-capped pretzel vendor opened the pretzel cabinet and warmed
his hands that smelled of dough and mustard and the inside of his old
coat-pockets. The hot air turned into a cloud of white to make the
salty taste almost visible. Further uptown in Central Park the horse-
drawn carriages carried laughing lovers and other children on a cir-
cular tour. Pieces of carols from many sources filled the air. A taxi
with a "Happy Holidays" sign on its hood honked furiously.

She was a fixture in the city's high-society scene. He would not
make the social register this or any year.

Inside the store, the volume of her "oohs and aahs" was directly
proportional to the prices on the tags. Finally, the grey-suited salesman with a sprig of holly in his lapel took her to a polished shelf of
transparent creatures, a glass menagerie. The salesman picked up a
six-hundred-dollar sparrow and handed it to her. "Just the thing," she
thought. But in her hands the bird was less a thing of beauty than a
trinket, a fulfillment of an obligation, a gift to someone who was
almost forgotten and who might get left off next year's list.

The sparrow sat noiselessly perched on her palm as she looked
up. When she did, her eyes glanced beyond the shelf of animals and
through the window onto Fifth Avenue. And there she caught sight
of his intent face through the lightly frosted glass. As if jabbed by the
umbrella-tip of reality, she shuddered at his look and the bird, for
one brief moment, took flight. Out it arced and she had no hope of
catching it. It shattered against the shelf and in breaking sang its first
song ever. She had bought it.

He withdrew from the window satisfied, having received the
best gift he could have from her hand, though it was clumsily given.
He ambled off downtown after adjusting the collar of his jacket. He
was stiff from the cold but felt as warm inside as the street-vendor's
hot pretzels.

※

Better than Perfect

*E*xcept for the erratic percussive accompaniment in the background, the carols sounded pure and clean over the loudspeaker system. Large metallic red letters spelling "Happy Holidays" hung from the ceiling between two boards bearing names and numbers: Joanna – 682, David – 740, and others. The alpha and omega points of decoration were the bright, red-bowed green wreaths secured to the walls at either end of the building beside lanes one and thirty-two. And there was an animated figure of Santa that stood in a corner of the childcare room waving and blinking and turning his head. The manager had forgotten to turn him off, and of course, there were no children in the room this day. They were other places.

It was Christmas Day at Ten Pin City. Fifty cents a game. Complimentary coffee. Bowls of nuts on every tabletop. Not exactly a place you'd call home for the holidays, but for the fifteen folks who had journeyed to this city of bowling, it was the alternative to being alone. And for Madge, who served as hostess, cook, waitress, cashier, and dishwasher at the alley's snack bar, it was where the manager had told her she would be. And that did not bother her at all; she'd be home in plenty of time to receive the one gift that mattered to her – a call from her granddaughter out East.

Almost everyone partook of the holiday special meal. Madge served up plates of sliced turkey, mashed potatoes, canned peas, and cranberry sauce. And she smothered it all, even the cranberry sauce, with a hot ladlefull of light brown gravy. "Compliments to the chef!" she heard from a plump woman who had put ketchup on her peas. Customers exchanged greetings at the counter and occasionally glanced over to observe those still bowling, still coaxing pins to fall with body-english. When there was an especially solid-sounding hit, all heads snapped to look. These were true bowlers who knew the sound of a strike. Two elderly men, both in plaid flannel shirts, took advantage of the mistletoe Madge had hung over the cash register. One blushed. Both left dollar tips tucked beneath plates cleaned of pumpkin pie.

Jake came in early in the afternoon. He ate two pieces of pie and said, "Those were pretty good, Madge." He looked at the mistletoe, decided to pass on the opportunity, and went straight to lane twelve. No one at the alley knew much about Jake other than that he was a handyman who worked alone and lived alone and seldom spoke. As a bowler he was, like Madge's pies, pretty good.

After limbering up, Jake rolled his first ball. It skidded a bit, then caught hold of the hardwood and hooked right into the pocket. A strike. With nobody sitting at the snack bar, no heads turned. Only Madge heard the distinctive thud of a perfect hit, and she smiled as she put dishes into the sink and began to wash. She had trained herself not to look up at the sounds of strikes. But still she heard them. Two, three, four, five from lane twelve. And then there stood Jake at the counter.

He said, "Pretty good start today." She said, "So I've heard." And he knew what she meant. "Do you want anything, Jake?" He looked embarrassed at the question and replied, "I guess I wanted to tell someone. But I'll take a glass of milk, too." Madge poured out the milk and Jake poured out more words than he'd spoken to one person in a long time. "Maybe I shouldn't have stopped. Maybe I should have kept going. Maybe I was on a hot streak. I've had six, seven in a row before but never at the start of a game. I didn't mean to bother you, and I don't mean to brag. There are lots of better bowlers than me…I guess I'll go back now. Can I leave the rest of the milk here?" Madge took it. "I'll keep it cold, but you stay hot."

Madge pretended to make coffee and to wipe down the soda machine. She was really watching Jake, feeling close to him and with him. Somehow Jake's awkwardness of speech had ill-prepared her for his grace with a bowling ball. She marveled. And each time he released it she could anticipate hearing the same sound again and again as it crushed into the pins. Six, seven, eight, nine strikes. And again he came to the counter. Madge handed him the milk and he looked beyond her.

"I do painting, plumbing, fixing things. And I'm pretty good, too. Never have done anything perfect though. You know what I mean?" Madge nodded. "Probably I shouldn't have stopped. Probably threw my rhythm off. Probably I'm wasting your time. I mean, it's really just between me and those pins." Madge lifted the empty glass from Jake's hand. Slowly she walked to the sink and began washing the glass deliberately. The sound from lane twelve was sweet. Strike. Madge turned to watch as Jake rubbed the ball and glided again toward the foul line. She broke into a smile when he released it. No doubt about it. Eleven strikes. So it came to one more roll. Madge clenched the wet glass tightly as though in fervent prayer. Jake let the ball go with the same flowing motion. It skidded, caught hold too quickly, and began a sharper hook. Madge reached for a towel and closed her eyes. The sound was different, lighter than the others. When she dared to look, Jake was on his way to the counter. Behind him she saw the seven and ten pins standing. Too much headpin. A split. Final score: 298.

Jake reached for the piece of pie Madge set before him.

"I wanted to be perfect," he said.

"Don't we all," Madge replied. Jake managed the trace of a smile.

"What was the point of it?" he asked.

Madge stared right at him and said simply, "The point of it was that I was with you."

"With me?" Jake softened, seeing that, yes, there was a point to that.

"I was with you every roll, the perfect ones, the one that wasn't. I even let the coffee pot run dry because I watched."

Jake forked in the remainder of the pie. The words came hard. "Thanks for being with me this Christmas. It's been better than pretty good."

❈

A Tale of Two Congregants

The Community Church had two members named Bob and Jeremy. The fact that both attended worship every Sunday was the only discernible thing they had in common. Bob came from a military background, prided himself on political conservatism, and displayed a competitive streak in sports that bordered on ruthlessness. Jeremy worked as a potter, voted Green Party, and pursued solitary activities like hiking. They had no friends in common. Jeremy's social companions were ragtag rabble in Bob's mind and the people Bob

called his business associates Jeremy referred to as capitalist preda-
tors. The pair did have something of a similar attitude toward attire,
for both of them used clothes to express their identity. Bob reveled
in the cut and look of his custom-made silk suits; Jeremy expressed
himself through the faded jeans he spent hours embroidering with
intricate patterns.

One spring, the church's nominating committee, in its infinite
wisdom (or desperation), put Bob and Jeremy on the board of deacons together. Without the relief of staggered terms, this slated
them to endure three years of contact. Though it turned out that
each of the deacons' meetings served to illustrate the radically different approaches of the two men, the sessions also underscored the
centrality of faith in both their lives. Then came the first time they
served communion together. All went well until the passing of the
chalice, which the deacons shared with one another. Jeremy served
Bob saying, "This is the blood of Christ, shed for you." Bob then took
the cup, drank, and as he prepared to serve Jeremy, transferred the
cup to his other hand. Doing that caused the cup to tilt, and wine
tumbled all over Jeremy's finest embroidered pants. Jeremy looked
down, and then extended his hand to receive the cup. Bob silently
gave it, took it back and spoke. "This is the blood of Christ," he
stated. Then he carefully poured a generous amount onto the leg of
his silk suit, looked Jeremy in the eyes, and said, "shed for you."

Such acts of humble, self-sacrificing love are tools of the Spirit
that open the way to reconciliation and understanding. Bob took
Jeremy to an Amvets dinner as his guest; Jeremy drove Bob to a lecture on boycotting as a consumer action. A friendship formed, and
both became involved with Amnesty International. They even
exchanged Bibles at one point to see which passages the other had
marked. They discussed the differences over Navy-strength coffee at
Bob's house or herb tea at Jeremy's place. Their mutual understandings grew, the spiritual products of humble, self-sacrificing love.

❄

Coffee Hour Communion

During a week of vacation, the Rev. Hadley decided to visit a
neighboring congregation for Sunday worship. This proved to be

immediately unsettling, for throughout the service there was a palpable chill that had nothing to do with the temperature of the air. She experienced the time of communion as a period of cold disconnection, and at the post-service coffee hour she felt a numbing uneasiness.

There was tension in the large parish hall room. Sure, people were chatting loudly, but there was no feel of community. The few wealthy people in the church clung together. A couple newcomers found backs turned toward them. Young people left the room. A group that the Rev. Hadley approached traded gossip and occasionally gestured at someone in the room. A few elderly folks sat separately and were not spoken to. The visiting minister thought she was the only one who noticed the disconnectedness, but she was wrong. A mentally retarded young man named Ruppert not only noticed, but being a wise and brave disciple, acted. He got more and more agitated and upset until tears formed in his eyes. Then he grabbed a tray full of fruit punch in Dixie cups, plopped a large handful of kids' cookies on the side and trudged across the room. He pressed the tray against the belly of one of the gossipers, looked him straight in the eye, and said in a loud voice, "Christ for you!" Needless to say, this got people's attention. For the next ten minutes the room was still and quiet as self-appointed deacon Ruppert made his rounds, the only voice being heard that of an increasingly happier young man perhaps speaking with the voice of God. It was a most holy communion, with Christ potently present. And it was a foundational community-building event for that church. The Rev. Hadley left with a prayer of thanksgiving in her heart.

❧

Baked and Broken for You

One activity that Kerry Johnson considered a sure-fire winner with his youth group was making bread, specifically Irish soda bread. It was relatively foolproof, had enough ingredients to keep many hands active, and tasted wonderful. One high school group he led had among its members two persons named James and Peter. Those disciples' names should not imply closeness between the two. The feeling that defined their relationship could only be described as the antithesis of fellowship...a sort of inexplicable and riling antagonism that manifested itself in pranks, plots and put-downs. Kerry found himself secretly wishing, upon occasion, that one or the other would be absent from a meeting. No such luck on bread-baking night.

As usual, James and Peter taunted one another while others tried to ignore them. They had to be reprimanded for shooting raisins at each other. Finally, though, every group member got his or her own portion of dough to place in a small bread pan...James hit first. Kerry watched as he casually went out to the gravel parking area for a breath of air. Upon return to the kitchen, he sauntered by Peter's unbaked loaf, dropped a small handful of raisin-sized pebbles into the mix, patted them out of sight, and came in to join the evening discussion. The ovens warmed to the proper temperature and group members popped the loaves inside. James could scarcely contain his glee. What he did not know was that in his absence out-doors, Peter had thumbed a hole in James' loaf, poured in half a bottle of lemon extract, and then covered the opening. Peter con-tributed to the discussion with smug seriousness.

The talk centered on what would be done with the loaves. A decision evolved. The young people decided that since bread was used in communion as a sign of fellowship and forgiveness, each person in the group would give his or her loaf to someone with whom reconciliation was needed. The meeting ended, but as the group members were leaving, Kerry noticed some raisins on the floor. "Peter and James," he said, "stay here a few minutes to pick up those raisins and to sponge the floor."

Upon completing the task in as uncooperative a manner as pos-sible, the boys picked up their loaves. Kerry asked, "Who are you going to give them to?" The boys looked at each other blankly. Then (in an action surely Spirit-inspired) they both extended the loaf to one another. Both were simultaneously touched and aghast. Kerry could not resist what he did next. He said, "That's beautiful. I think you should sit down right now, break bread together, and eat your fill. In fact, I insist." James ate delicately. Peter chewed with a puck-ering smile. Both confronted their own misdeeds in the eating of those loaves. It was a gloriously holy communion. And Christ was truly present in the sharing of that bread.

✳

Broken Bread for the Common Flock

On a crisp fall day, Cheryl decided to take a walk through a small city park near her apartment. There were the usual joggers, several newspaper readers, a few picnickers. Around one park bench inhabited by a thin grayish man, there was an undulating feather carpet – hundreds of bobbing birds. The fellow had a large garbage bag beside him, and from it he withdrew piece after piece of bread. These he reduced to crumbs and tossed gently to the ground. Without asking permission to enter this scene, Cheryl slowly walked around the birds and sat on the opposite end of the bench from the feeder.

"You must like birds," he said. "Yes, I do," Cheryl replied. "Me, too." "Where'd you get all that bread?" she inquired. "From the dumpster behind the market, the dumpster near the high rise, the dumpster behind Wendy's. Perfectly good stuff." He paused. "It's the same I eat. Me and my flock. Same bread. Help yourself." Cheryl blanched and said, "Thank you. I just ate. But I'll feed these guys." Soon she had a pecking mob around her feet. "You probably noticed," said the bread man. "What?" "They're all pigeons and sparrows. Amazing, huh?" He went on. "Worthless birds. Nuisance birds. Common birds. Who cares about pigeons and sparrows? But I do. We have a lot in common. So we eat together. I give 'em everything I can gather." He stopped to button his jacket, to pull up its collar. Cheryl looked at him with great respect. Here he was, eking out an existence on the fringe of society and his first thought was to provide for the least among the creatures of the park. From subsistence living he gave of his substance.

Cheryl turned away with tears in her eyes knowing she had much more to learn about generosity and compassion. He tossed handful after handful of crumbs. And Christ was present in the sharing of that bread.

※

Grace Juice

One day during her vacation, Geri strolled to the beautiful downtown of the coastal village where she was staying. She bought a chocolate croissant and sat in front of the bakery watching the scene around her. Her attention was drawn to a child of about two years who was thoroughly enjoying a box of animal crackers and a small bottle of fruit juice. Her mother sat beside her on a bench talking rapidly to an older couple who had stopped to see the child. Geri tried engaging the attention of the little girl but couldn't compete with the excitement of traffic and passersby, so she lapsed into listening to Mom. Within seconds of tuning into Mother's monologue, Geri learned that the child's name was Jeanine. And within a matter of minutes more, she learned that Jeanine had an IQ substantially into the genius range and would be afforded every opportunity by her parents to develop every bit of potential crammed into her little being. Mom talked on and on about Jeanine's astonishing scores in infant intelligence tests, about her psychosocial maturity level, about her advanced fine motor skills. The only time Mother stopped talking was when she reached into a large leather handbag that hung over the back of her chair. She withdrew a cigarette and lighter, lit up, and dropped the lighter back inside.

Geri didn't know whether to be in awe of Jeanine or to feel sorry for her. As her mother began talking about researching proper educational enhancement opportunities, Geri settled on sorry. Then, just as Geri was about to get up and move on, Jeanine took her bottle of fruit juice and poured a tentative amount into Mom's handbag. This action was obscured from the couple's view by the stroller and from Mother's view by her inattention. Jeanine peeked in the pocketbook and smiled. Instinct made Geri lean forward to say something, however, just as she prepared to speak, she heard Mother rambling on about Jeanine's advanced deductive capabilities. So Geri sat back and kept silent, for certainly the juice-pouring had been carefully thought out by the child and she wanted to observe the grand design unfold. Jeanine tipped about a quarter bottle into the handbag. A clever plan to thwart Mom's smoking habit, Geri decided. Jeanine smiled in Geri's direction and gobbled a couple crackers.

Mom crushed out her cigarette and Geri figured it would be a matter of minutes before she reached in for another, so she got up and left. Geri decided she didn't want to see the form Mother's delight would take when she discovered the clever way Jeanine had combined her fine motor skills and her deductive powers. A half-block away, Geri had to laugh out loud. She wished she could have hugged Jeanine. The little girl had given her the perfect example of why having the spirit of a child leads toward finding the reign and realm of God. Geri reminded herself that whenever we get too smug and self-certain, such spirit proclaims that life abounds with surprises, that our attempts to control are as all wet as the interior of Mom's handbag. By grace we live and move and have our being. Jeanine had poured out a daily portion of grace juice.

✢

Pond Life

Jeremy, at eleven years old, was already a skilled angler. He would fish anywhere, but his favorite spot was Daisy Pond where large bass cruised under the lily pads and rolled in the shallows where their light bellies flashed on the surface.

One of the best things about Daisy Pond was that even when the fish weren't biting it was a good place to be. Not a building could be seen from anyplace on its shore. The only signs of human life were a battered, rusty-green litter can and old Mr. Chadbourne's rowboat. Jeremy had been in that boat quite a few times and always listened carefully to Mr. Chadbourne, who had taught him how to tie strong knots on the line, how to stalk fish and to tease them into striking.

Daisy Pond was always alive. That is what Jeremy loved. Muskrats churned through the waters, porcupines wandered the nearby woods, turtles sat on rocks doing nothing much at all. The air sounded with insect hum and frog noises, splashes of feeding fish and a chorus of bird songs.

On one evening at sunset, just as the water shined pink and violet, Jeremy looked out over the pond. High above, a lone hawk soared in wide circles. And just above the water a whole flock of tree swallows darted about snatching insect-dinner from the air. The birds swerved and swooped as they ate their fill. Jeremy reeled in his line. He smiled at the birds' acrobatics.

Suddenly a most surprising thing happened. One of the birds misjudged its speed or became more hungry than careful, and it crashed – splat – right into the calm water of Daisy Pond. Jeremy leaned his fishing pole against a tree and watched with a heavy feeling. The little bird was a good forty feet from land. It chirped in terror at first and spun in one spot. Then it fell silent, and amazingly, using its wings as flippers, began ever so slowly moving toward the nearest shore. Jeremy couldn't believe his eyes. He silently started to root for the bird to make it.

The rest of the flock had stopped its insect-catching and now hovered all around their companion chirping encouragement. Jeremy tried to think of ways to help. "If I throw a branch I might hit it. The rowboat would scare it. And I can't swim out there. All I can do is hope and pray." The little bird continued on. It seemed to Jeremy that when it had gotten almost halfway to the shore it slowed down. "Worn out, I guess," Jeremy thought to himself. "Never going to make it. Some big bass will snatch it for dinner or maybe that hawk will dive down." But the hawk was uninterested, no fish struck, and the little bird continued on. The flock stayed just overhead.

"Come on, little guy!" Jeremy shouted. He wished that he were God and could pluck the swallow up to safety. The flock stuck by. Jeremy hoped and prayed. The little bird continued on.

Finally, it reached a dry log and shakily stood up on it. The flock shot up and away after insects. Jeremy put his fingers to his lips and let out a loud whistle.

And the little swallow sat on the log, a small drenched triumph of life over death.

✢

Plastic Grace

Marsha had made it in the corporate world. A fine salary. A beautifully decorated office with a solid cherry desk. A splendid reputation among her peers as someone who paid careful attention to details. One early evening at the end of a full workday, Marsha sat at her desk opening mail. As she did, she glanced at the picture of her husband, son, and daughter, a picture that served as the only decoration on a surface that was otherwise all business. She thought happily about seeing them soon when the 6:47 PM train pulled into the station. The three of them were proud of Marsha's accomplishments, and they were her pride and joy.

The final envelope she slit open was the monthly account of her MasterCard purchases, and she scanned the figures with practiced ease. All correct...but for one. The most recent. A $6.98 charge to a drugstore way uptown. In an instant, Marsha panicked. Over a week before, she had dropped her wallet on the platform just as the train was rolling to a stop. Her credit cards had slid out and a pleasant young man in coveralls had helped her scoop them up. She had assumed they were all there. Marsha Stone, stickler for details, had made an assumption, a wrong one as it turned out. The MasterCard was gone, all right, and with a feeling of anger directed at her for being so careless, Marsha phoned the toll-free number to cancel the card. While she waited for a customer service person to help her, she noticed that though the billing period on the statement ran to the end of the month, the only charge made by the thief had been on the 26th. In almost a week of use, just one $6.98 purchase. When someone came on the phone to offer assistance, Marsha asked, "Is it possible for you to find out exactly what item the charge of August 26th at Granger's Pharmacy covered?" "Probably so, ma'am. If the store kept a record. It might take a few days. Is anything wrong, ma'am?" Marsha thought about her $20,000 line of credit, sighed, and said, "I hope not."

Eight days later Marsha got her answer. "Liniment," said the voice on the phone. Marsha looked at the phone and then replied, "I beg your pardon." "On your MasterCard. Liniment. A $6.98 charge for liniment. Sore muscle stuff. Do you remember now?" "Oh, yes. That's fine." Marsha hung up the phone and wrote out a check to pay her MasterCard bill. Weeks later, when the September one arrived, she opened it almost breathlessly before all other mail. Two charges caught her attention. One for $83.00 at a large food market, one for $56.00 at a discount children's clothing store. A MasterCard service person reported that the latter purchase included three boys' shirts, a jumper, and two pairs of tights. School clothes. "Everything O.K.?" he asked. "Yes, yes. Perfectly O.K." Marsha mailed off a check the next day. For October, there were three charges. On the 14th, there was $26.00 to a florist and $32.00 to an Italian restaurant. Marsha guessed an anniversary. Later in the month, a repeat $6.98 at Granger's Pharmacy.

Marsha was piecing together a picture of her newfound friends…an uptown family of four, one or both parents having jobs that required physical labor, two young children – a boy and a girl. She found herself becoming fond of them, intimately bound to them as she was by a delicate mutual trust. In November, Marsha noted a pre-Thanksgiving supermarket charge of $17.54, for a turkey, she suspected, and $88.00 at a place called Jadwin's. The MasterCard man did his research and said, "Tires, ma'am. Specifically, two winter retreads. Surely you remember." "Of course." He continued. "I don't mean to be nosy, but I noticed on charges earlier this year that you own a BMW. Really, ma'am, you shouldn't put retreads on a Beemer." Marsha replied, "They're for my second car." And in a way, that was true.

Before the December charge arrived, Marsha knew it would be just for toys. What was unexpected was a card addressed just to her. It contained a picture of the infant Jesus and a handwritten message: "Your Master and ours. Thank you." Two small photos, school pictures, were taped to the card. Marsha held them and read the neatly printed words: "I love you. Jolene." "Merry Christmas! Richard." Her extension of plastic grace had enriched her in a way no business deal had ever done. The next day, one of Marsha's co-workers noticed the two small pictures tucked into the corners of the frame on her desk. "Who are they?" Marsha could think of no easy explanation, so she answered honestly, "Family."

❈

Robins in the Rafters

Since it was drizzling lightly, Jamie ended up with his driver and bucket of golf balls in one of the roofed stalls at the driving range. After warming up, he hit the first half-dozen balls from the large wire container: sliced two, nailed two, knocked one into a pond, and ricocheted one off the 100-yard sign. As he teed up again, he heard a sound close above his head. "Cheep-cheep. Cheep-cheep." He looked up and saw a parent robin stuffing some sort of squirmy food into the mouths of three nestlings. The nest itself was built on one of the rafters that supported the roof of the driving shed...inches away from the arc of a whizzing club head. Jamie considered moving, but all the other covered tees were in use, and for a moment he wondered what had induced the robins to set up house-keeping in such a precarious place. Had they mistaken the buckets for nests full of eggs? Yet if so, why hadn't they been deterred by what folks did to those eggs? Had they heard people talking happily about birdies? Yet if so, why hadn't they been apprehensive about even more gleeful comments about those predatory eagles? Jamie concluded that Mr. and Mrs. Robin were simply birdbrains who had given the matter little consideration. "What a spot to raise a family," he thought to himself as he prepared to take a whack at ball number seven.

For the next twenty minutes, try as he did, Jamie couldn't keep his attention on golf. It kept getting diverted to the robins. He began to take note of certain things. The parents would time their entries and exits to coincide with his bending down to tee up a ball. Never did they take flight during a swing. Always, they departed to the rear, avoiding potential collisions with balls. Jamie watched Mom and Dad pluck worms and grubs from the conveniently located, well-watered greens nearby. He observed that for his club to reach the nest during a swing, he would have to take his follow-through smack through the lower part of a two-by-six crossbeam. He noticed that the baby birds stayed nice and dry during the shower. He listened as they continued to sing a cheery "cheep-cheep, cheep-cheep," amidst the chaotic sounds of solid hits and miss-hits, clatters and curses and grunts. Slowly he began to develop a deep appreciation and respect for the robins in the rafters, and even grew to feel a kinship with them. He glanced upward at the nest, alive with tending, eating and singing, and said aloud, "Yup, life's like that." Duffers to the left and to the right doing scary things. All present security tenuous. Yet in spite of the danger and fragility, life asserts itself through daily activity as something bountiful and growing and good. Worthy a glad song. Cheep-cheep.

❋

The Voice of the Bread

Jenny had just moved into the suburbs. Her new job drew her there, and the promise of a living wage lured her to this area of affluence. On Saturday, she emptied her car of all worldly belongings, filled one of the three rooms in her apartment, and settled in. On Sunday, she donned her best dress, a $3.00 Goodwill special, and headed off to church.

As Jenny walked up the steps, she marveled at the manicured shrubbery, the scrubbed stones, the polished brass, and the manicured-scrubbed-and-polished people. At her best, she was easily the worst-dressed attendee. An usher handed her a program, grudgingly she thought, and she sat down in a pew where a slight shift slid her inches along the shiny wood. She remained prayerfully still and noticed that nobody sat near her.

The place made Jenny feel uncomfortable. She imagined that spiders attempting to spin webs in the uppermost rafters would be dealt with murderously, and she began to wonder how severely she would be dealt with for having mildly scuffed shoes. The service itself had a well-rehearsed quality. The choir sang flawlessly. The organist played a magnificent instrument in such a way as to drown out any imperfections in congregational singing. No coins clattered in the collection plates. And the minister, almost certainly a model from *Gentlemen's Quarterly,* delivered a sermon that Jenny considered over-polite spiritual fluff. Yet it was delivered in fine round tones.

Throughout the service, Jenny kept looking at the communion table, set up with a vast array of ornate and glistening antique silver. Perhaps she looked there out of her own hunger and thirst, perhaps in unknowing anticipation of the miracle that would happen there that day. It took place just after the minister intoned Jesus' words, "This is my body which is broken for you." He raised the symbolic loaf and pulled from the ends so it would halve neatly where it had been pre-sliced part-way through. But nothing happened. The designated pre-slicer had slipped up. The minister's eyes showed panic; then he gave a sharp strong tug. In the silence of the church, the loaf POPPED apart. It was as though the Bread of Life had uttered a groan. The building's perfect acoustics carried the sound to every-one in the pews, and there came a collective congregational gasp. The minister, frozen, held aloft the jagged-edged pieces of bread. They spoke silent volumes about the sacrificial quality of Christian love, and they extended swift forgiveness to the negligent loaf-slicer. The minister said, "Do this in remembrance of me," and those words had new meaning. The POP had been a joyful sound, a revelatory sound, good news to all who heard it of God's sometimes intrusive, soul-shaking, always loving presence. Jenny felt at home.

※

Love as a Slam-Dunk

On a summer trip last year, Rasheed went to Battery Park on New York harbor. There he saw a tourist couple hand their son a ten-dollar bill. They told him, "This is for ice cream now, and the rest you can use to buy a toy or a souvenir at the Statue of Liberty." The father then accompanied the boy, age six or so, over to the short line at the ice cream truck. Just after the child purchased some multi-colored frozen concoction on a stick, he noticed a homeless man rummaging through the trash next to a hot dog vendor's wagon. The man pulled out a small unfinished bag of potato chips and smiled when he shook a soda can to find it almost half full. The boy stared and stood frozen in his tracks. "Look how hungry he is," he said. Father replied, "Right," and put his hand on his son's shoulder to direct his attention away and to get him moving.

Tears formed on the boy's face and an idea formed in a flash. Before his father could grab him, the child darted away, and with the decisiveness of a Shaquille O'Neal shot, slam-dunked every bill and coin in his possession smack into the homeless man's hand. The star-tled fellow dropped a couple coins, scurried after them, then walked boldly to the back of the hot dog vendor's line. The boy's parents did not know what to say when they reconvened at a bench. "Now you don't have any money to spend," seemed obvious and irrelevant. "Don't ever do that again," seemed stupid, especially since Mom was now crying at her son's kindness. Finally the boy spoke through lips smeared pink, green and purple, "I couldn't help it. I had to give it to him. He was hungry." The parents were wise enough to hug him rather than reprimand, and they suspected that the boy would be taking back home the souvenir memory of an act of Godly giving. Rasheed left Battery Park with a new understanding of the righteous recklessness of love.

❊

A Birth Announcement

Rebecca and Pat had become best friends soon after they moved to the same area of town within months of one another. Both were mystery readers and gardeners, both had grown up near Boston and were delighted with the shift to a rural area, both were mothers of three — two boys and a girl for Rebecca, two girls and a boy for Pat — but most of all, both were singers of considerable talent. Twenty years or so back when they were first in town they dual-handedly renewed the village church's choir. With their singing came a fresh interest and an energy that helped the church come alive with music.

Then, some time ago, came The Feud. Although neither person could remember exactly what started it, Pat was pretty certain it began with an insult at a party and Rebecca was fairly sure it had its origins in a difference over garden tools. Whatever the case, as this feud grew from not talking to one another to talking destructively about one another, the people affected by it grew in number. Rebecca's and Pat's husbands no longer went hunting together; the kids were prohibited from playing together. The local nurseryman was accused by both of selling choicer seedlings to the other. And all the town's social events were contrived to prevent a confrontation.

Nowhere was the tension more felt than in the village church. The choir had been the last battleground before The Feud entered its present lengthy stage of seething and separation. For months after the outbreak of hostilities, Rebecca and Pat had tried to outdo one another in the choir's presentations. Sunday anthems turned into duets, duets into vocal duels. Two beautiful soprano voices used as weapons just about killed the choir. One Sunday neither Rebecca nor Pat showed up to sing. The next week Pat came to church and sat in the second pew from the front on the right; Rebecca placed herself in the second pew from the rear on the left. For years upon years the seating remained just so.

As time went by The Feud disturbed the peace of the church as others took sides. It was continued more out of stubbornness than intention; neither Pat nor Rebecca would consider making an apology or seeking reconciliation for fear of appearing weak or at fault. There seemed no way of saving them, the church, and the town from the effects of The Feud.

Then one Christmas Eve, Pat came late to the church service. Because the entire town showed up for that occasion, the place was jammed. Only one remaining space was ample enough to squeeze Pat in. The young usher nervously escorted her to that seat by the aisle... next to Rebecca.

For icy minutes through the scripture reading, both stared straight ahead, though feeling the eyes of the other. The prayer message got blocked out by the internal noise of discomfort within them. Then it was time to sing. The old urge to compete, to outdo, welled up in their voices and at the first refrain the rest of the congregation became mere background for two sopranos singing lovelessly: "This, this, is Christ the King, Whom shepherds guard and angels sing: Haste, haste to bring him laud, The babe, the son of Mary."

For the second refrain, Pat and Rebecca both determined to attack it with all they had and both hit the opening note full volume. And in this the miracle happened. Both came out with a sound so exquisitely bad, so stunningly flat, that their heads snapped toward one another as though they had been jabbed by a boxer. And within the span of a measure, those wrong notes reminded them each of their own fallibility. Beyond that very flat D no further confession of fault was needed. And wincing at the sounds they had made this night and for years, Rebecca and Pat began to laugh. With the multitude watching, two women embraced and sang with renewed joy of a child who, it has been said, can make warfare to cease.

※

Daybreak

Early morning. Early spring.
Light comes to the earth's lip, a taste of day's dawn.
Coffee comes to my lips, a sip of brewed awakening.
This time alone – the furnace still asleep at its nighttime set-
    ting,
the dog unmoving among the muddy boots piled in the
    pantry—
 I sit in a chair that sighs as I settle.
Outside, a few crows caw plots of thievery. They are
    like noisy shadows, dark harbingers of tomorrow's troubles.
Outside, thawed soil has recently endured the overturning
    blades. It
curls back upon itself row upon row, open and receptive.
I drain the cup and pause, struck by the fullness of gratitude
    within me.
In spirit I am myself a lengthening day, a land furrowed and
    ready.
And there is work to be done.

ℐNDEX